A SAINSBURY COOKBOOK

COOKING
—THE—
MEXICAN WAY

LOURDES NICHOLS

D1103754

CONTENTS

Published exclusively for J Sainsbury plc
Stamford House Stamford Street
London SE1 9LL
by Martin Books
Simon & Schuster International Group
Fitzwilliam House 32 Trumpington Street
Cambridge CB2 1QY

First published 1983
New enlarged edition 1985
Third impression 1989

ISBN 0 85941 490 6

Printed in Great Britain

THE AUTHOR

Lourdes Nichols was born in Mexico City and has lived in England for the last seventeen years. She began cooking at an early age, learning from her mother, who also helped her in compiling the recipes in this book.

When she first came to England Lourdes found it difficult to adapt her native Mexican recipes to the ingredients then available, although the choice of produce has improved considerably since. For the past six years she has been seriously involved in researching and teaching Mexican cookery.

Lourdes now divides her time between teaching, writing and catering for parties at the Mexican Embassy, Mexican Tourist Board and elsewhere, as well as running a small commercial tortilla-making business and a shop selling imported Mexican ingredients. She is a recognised authority on Mexican cuisine and has been featured on radio and television.

Lourdes lives in the Home Counties with her English husband and their three teenage children, who she says have been very encouraging and willing to try endless recipes!

INTRODUCTION

Mexican food has taken the United States by storm in recent years and looks set to be equally popular in Great Britain. Although so far it has been mainly available here as take-away 'fast food', it is easy to cook in the kitchen at home and the result is far more likely to resemble genuine Mexican cooking.

It is not hard to see why Mexican food is becoming so popular: colourful and exciting, delicious and filling, exotic yet wholesome and economical, it is equally suited to family meals or dinner parties. A little meat often goes a long way in Mexican dishes, with a lot of the protein coming from beans and vegetables; this makes it not only very economical but also healthy. Although it can be spicy, most of the ingredients are familiar foods available anywhere and the 'hotness' can be adjusted easily to suit every taste. Preparation methods are very simple and many of the recipes will freeze very well for reheating at a later date – especially useful for modern lifestyles.

Note on quantities

Ingredients in the recipes are given in both imperial (oz, pints, etc) and metric (g, ml, etc) measures: use either set of quantities, but not a mixture of both, in any one recipe. All spoons are level unless otherwise stated; metric spoon measures are always level. Egg size, where unspecified, is medium (size 3).

NB I have not given instructions in the recipes for removing seeds for chillies and peppers, since whether you remove them or not depends on how hot you want the dish to be – see notes on chillies.

What is the Mexican style of cookery? Many people would immediately think of tortillas (corn pancakes), beans and hot chilli flavouring as typical features. Although it is true that these ingredients, especially the tortillas, crop up often, I hope to show you in this book that there is much more than that to Mexican cuisine. A more important characteristic is the pride of place occupied by fresh vegetables and fruit. In nutritional terms, these contain a lot of health-giving vitamins and dietary fibre, which is one of the reasons that Mexican cookery fits in so well with modern ideas of a healthy diet.

The cooking in Mexico has been influenced by various European cuisines – Spanish, obviously, and to a lesser extent French – but its basis is still the native style, which goes back to the Aztecs and derives from the country's abundance of natural foods. Turkeys, peanuts, tomatoes, sweetcorn, avocados, pumpkins, courgettes, marrows, pineapples, many kinds of beans, chillies, chocolate and vanilla are all native products of Mexico that were introduced to Europe after the Spanish conquest; all of them feature again and again in Mexican dishes. The Aztecs used to cook their food by boiling, steaming or roasting over a wood fire. After the Spaniards introduced the pig and its much-appreciated fat, frying became a popular method. Ovens were almost unknown and are not common in Mexican kitchens even now; however, I have adapted recipes where necessary to take account of the conveniences of a modern British kitchen – oven and blender rather than open fire and pestle-and-mortar!

A typical day's meals in Mexico today would begin with a breakfast of fresh fruit juice, eggs cooked in many different ways accompanied by warm tortillas or fresh bread, and black coffee or chocolate. That is in the cities; in the countryside the peasants will go to work at dawn after a meal of black coffee and tortillas, returning at about ten o'clock for almuerzo (brunch), consisting of eggs, beans, tortillas and more coffee. The humble peasant needs no plates or cutlery but wraps his food in a freshly made, warm tortilla, and even the most sophisticated and affluent town–dweller will eat his tortilla the traditional way, 'by hand'.

The main meal everywhere is in the middle of the day, at around two o'clock. A typical lunch would include soup, 'dry soup' (rice or pasta in sauce), meat with one vegetable, beans, salad, and fruit or dessert accompanied by black coffee. (Mexican cookery is not noted for its desserts: although the Spaniards introduced milk and sugar, fresh tropical fruit is still the typical light, sweet end to a meal.) Tortillas are offered throughout this succession of courses, as well as some sort of salsa (sauce) to make tacos with (see page 67). In some homes white bread, usually freshly baked and resembling small French rolls, called bolillos or teleras, is offered. Agua fresca (cool, fruit–flavoured water) is always available.

After such a heavy lunch, supper is a light

5

meal. Served at about eight or nine o'clock, it usually takes the form of an antojito (a 'little whim', i.e. whatever takes your fancy). Beans with soft tortillas or sweet bread and hot chocolate or coffee are very popular.

In this book I have provided a sample of typically Mexican recipes which I am sure will turn you into an enthusiast for this exciting national cuisine. They are all my personal versions of genuine Mexican dishes, with just the occasional ingredient adapted to what is available in Britain. They range from starters to desserts, and I have included some suggestions for authentic Mexican drinks.

Ingredients

Exact combinations of ingredients have never been a feature of the Mexican cuisine. Because it is centuries old and has been passed down from one generation to another by word of mouth, small changes and adjustments have always been the accepted norm. The amounts of salt, black pepper, chillies and some spices given in the recipes in this book are only a rough guide, for my aim is to inspire you to experiment and do what tastes right to you. After all, that is half the fun of cooking – especially Mexican cooking!

Avocados *(Aguacates)* Avocados come in many different sizes, colours and textures. In Mexico they are available the whole year round. The small, black-skinned ones that resemble a large plum are my favourites.

Avocados are eaten hot only when dropped into soup before serving, or when made into avocado soup. The use of fresh coriander and lime with them accentuates their mild flavour.

Always remember to buy avocados at least five days in advance during the winter months; in the summer months, two or three days ahead will be sufficient. Avocados sold in Britain are not normally ripe enough to eat the same day.

You can tell that an avocado is ripe when it gives slightly, like a peach, if pressed gently between your fingers. To ripen, wrap in newspaper and keep in a warm room or airing cupboard. Check daily, turning round for even ripening. If an avocado seems ripe before you are ready to use it, you may delay its maturity by placing it in the vegetable compartment of your refrigerator.

Beans *(Frijoles)* Beans are pulses of different colours and sizes which constitute the main source of protein in the Mexican diet. They are rich in minerals and protein and are eaten at every meal. Amongst the better known in Britain are the red kidney beans. They must first be soaked to allow them to swell and soften and then boiled at a rolling boil until very soft; this can take 2–3 hours.

In Mexico beans are cooked in an earthenware pot and are boiled continuously for up to 3 hours. Boil for at least 15 minutes to extract the substances which can cause stomach pains. Always check to ensure they are boiling in sufficient water, enough to cover them at least 2 inches (5 cm) over the top. Never add cold water to boiling beans or the result will be frijoles parados – 'standing-up beans' – which are indigestible and unpalatable.

Beans are a tasty and economical way of feeding the family. One pound (450 g) of dried beans yields approximately 3 lb (1.3 kg) of cooked beans. Beans are amongst the most popular dishes in Mexico and together with maize and chillies they make a happy trio satisfying daily protein, carbohydrate and vitamin C requirements.

It is advisable not to serve more than one bean dish at each meal, as beans cause flatulence and can make some people extremely uncomfortable. However, the more often you eat them the less they have this effect on you.

Chillies *(Chiles)* Chillies are eaten both raw and cooked. Their pungency is variable, but some are so hot that they will irritate your fingers (or your eyes, if you rub them with your fingers) for days. To avoid getting 'hot fingers' you should wear rubber gloves or use a knife and fork to handle chillies; chop them on an absorbent kitchen towel.

To control the amount of 'sting' in your dish follow these simple rules:

(a) For mild dishes do not prick or puncture a chilli; leave it whole. Remove chillies from dishes immediately after the cooking is finished.

(b) For medium-hot dishes, add several whole chillies, then slice only one lengthways, discarding the seeds.

(c) For hot dishes, add sliced chillies, seeds and all. Keep in mind that not everyone has the same tolerance and once your dish is 'hot' there is little you can do to make it mild. Taste as you add more chillies so that you know when to stop.

(d) For use in uncooked dishes, like Salcita and Guacamole (page 22), I generally chop the chillies as fine as I can so that when they are mixed with the other ingredients no one will get an overdose!

To be on the safe side, I always prepare 'pickled peppers' (see page 31) and place them on the table separately, while keeping the chillies actually cooked in the dish to a minimum. In this way each person can regulate the amount they dare take. If you have never been exposed to chillies and would like to try them, all I can say is take a little piece of chilli at a time with a forkful of food.

To keep chillies, remove the stalks carefully so that you do not break the fruit, wrap the fruit in absorbent kitchen paper and refrigerate in an airtight container. They will keep well for about two weeks. Do not freeze chillies.

Recipes calling for Mexican varieties of dry chillies have deliberately been avoided because they are difficult to obtain in this country. However, for the sake of authenticity I have included them in the recipe for Mole (page 78).

The basic ingredients of Mexican cooking are colourful and healthy, with a strong emphasis on pulses and fresh vegetables

Coriander *(Cilantro)*   Coriander is used fresh in all recipes in this book (coriander seeds are seldom used in Mexican cooking). It is a herb which looks like parsley and is usually sold with its roots. It has such a distinct flavour when eaten raw that there is really no substitute for it. However, alternative herbs are possible in cooked dishes and I have specified these in the recipes.

Coriander keeps best wrapped in absorbent paper, and refrigerated in an airtight container it will keep for about ten days. If it seems a little limp, soak it in cold water for an hour, or remove the leaves from the stalks and soak them for 30 minutes before using. Do not freeze.

BASIC RECIPES

Certain basic dishes are required again and again as ingredients or components of many of the recipes in this book. I have put them together in this section, to make them easier to find if you are preparing them fresh for a particular dish. However, I recommend you save time by making up a larger quantity and freezing for future use as needed (only the raw tomato sauce, page 22, cannot be stored in this way).

Tortillas are the basis of very many recipes. Cooked or re-fried beans can be used both as ingredients and as accompanying dishes in their own right, as can the savoury minced beef recipe. The two tomato sauces, the avocado dip and the spicy chorizo sausage are delicious and versatile ingredients. The Mexican-style chicken stock is a marvellous base for Mexican soups.

TORTILLAS

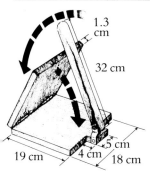

1.3 cm

32 cm

19 cm   4 cm   5 cm   18 cm

Tortilla was the name given by the Spaniards to the flat corn pancakes eaten by the Indians in Mexico. The primitive name was *tlaxcali*, because it was the Indians from the township of Tlaxcala who made them originally. Tortillas made the traditional way are patted by hand, one at a time, and lots of patience and rhythm are essential to keep the dough from folding or, indeed, dropping on the ground! Tortilla presses are a wonderfully simple solution to those of us who cannot get the rhythm right. They are used in many Mexican homes to speed up the process of tortilla making and are practical even if you only use them occasionally – though with practice a lot more can be achieved. Although tortillas can now be bought ready-made in some shops, it is fun to make your own. The diagram shows how easy it is to make a press for home use.

Tortillas must never be eaten cold, unless they are deep-fried and used as corn chips, called *totopos*. In every other case you should warm tortillas before serving them. They are most commonly eaten with savoury fillings, but are also offered to children warm with butter and sugar. They are used for appetisers, in soups and main courses and they take the place of bread at each meal. You need never throw a tortilla away, because there is always some use for a stale one.

I have provided two recipes for tortillas. The first one is for the traditional corn tortilla, for which you will need maize flour or *masa harina*: this is now available over here in speciality shops. The second recipe is for the rarer, but still authentic, wheat flour version, which uses ingredients that are more familiar and easier to come by in Britain. When you make tortillas, make a large batch and freeze plenty for future use.

TORTILLAS DE MAIZ

(Corn tortillas)   Makes approx. 30 tortillas, 6 inches (15 cm) in diameter

1¼ lb (550 g) masa harina (maize flour)

4 oz (100 g) plain white flour

1 pint (600 ml) hot water

Corn tortillas are round, flat unleavened pancakes made of a mixture of specially prepared cornmeal and water. They are traditionally patted by hand until they are wafer-thin, then cooked on a hot griddle without grease or fat. In Mexico tortillas are bought by the kilo at the tortillerías *but in Britain they are harder to find. They are available frozen or canned from speciality shops, but it is more satisfying to make your own.*

This recipe must be followed exactly, otherwise you may find it very difficult to make the tortillas. If your first batch isn't entirely successful, persevere, making sure that you are keeping to the recipe; it's worth the trouble. A tortilla press is essential and you will need also a griddle or thick-bottomed frying pan and 40 squares of waxed paper, about 8 × 8 inches (20 × 20 cm).

Place a heavy frying pan or griddle on a medium heat and warm until a drop of water in it sizzles. In the meantime, mix the flours and add the water gradually, mixing as you go along. Knead as for bread, for 5 minutes with an electric mixer or 10 minutes by hand; you cannot over-knead the masa. You will know the dough is ready when a small ball placed in a glass of cold water does not dissolve.

Take 1 heaped tablespoon (2 × 15 ml spoon) of dough and mould it into a small ball in the palm of your hands (1). Open the tortilla press and place one square of waxed paper on the base of it, waxed side up.

Place the dough ball in the centre of the paper, a little nearer the bracket than the centre (2). Now put another square of waxed paper, waxed side down, over it. Fold the tortilla press down on it and apply pressure on the lever, gently pressing with your right hand and holding the top of the lever with your left hand (3).

Open the press and check the thickness of the tortilla: it should be no thicker than a penny (4).

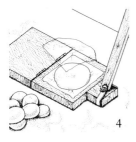

If it is too thick, close the press again and apply a little more pressure, turning the tortilla around a quarter turn. Peel off the top layer of paper, and hold the tortilla in your hand with the other layer of paper. Place it face down on the hot griddle and leave it for about a minute, when you may peel the paper off and save it to re-use later.

When the tortilla is cooked, the sides will start lifting. Turn it over and cook for half a minute, then turn a third time, pressing gently in the centre so that it bubbles up. Remove it from the heat and stack it with the other cooked tortillas, covered with a clean kitchen towel. They are now ready to eat, freeze or refrigerate.

Hints: If the tortillas come out of the press with ragged edges, the dough is too dry. Add a little more water to the dough, knead it a little longer, then try again. If the tortilla is too difficult to flatten, the same applies.

When the dough is too wet, the tortilla becomes very sticky; it will make a lot of bubbles when placed on the griddle and often will stick. Add a little more masa harina and knead a little longer until your hands are clean.

If the tortillas crack when cooked, the griddle is too cold; if they get black spots, the griddle is too hot. Cool it down by placing a saucepan of cold water over it.

To refrigerate: allow the tortillas to cool and then wrap them in a plastic bag, tying them securely with a freezer wire. Can be stored in a refrigerator for about one week.

To freeze: wrap in a plastic bag, securely sealed, and place in a freezer; they will store for up to six months. They do not need to be thawed before use, as they do not stick together and so can easily be separated with the end of a knife and put straight on to a hot griddle. They will keep in a refrigerator for a week after thawing.

To reheat: if you only need a few, warm up a griddle or heavy-bottomed frying pan until water sizzles on it. Place one tortilla on the griddle or pan at a time and heat for about 30 seconds on each side. Keep the tortillas warm in a clean napkin and serve as soon as possible.

If you need to warm up a lot of tortillas simultaneously, then make small parcels of 12 tortillas each, wrapped securely in aluminium foil. Place the parcels in a medium-hot oven (Gas Mark 5/375°F/190°C) for 15 minutes. Alternatively, bring the water in a double boiler to the boil and place all the wrapped tortillas in it, cover and allow to steam for 12 minutes. For microwave heating, wrap two tortillas in a cloth napkin and warm at high setting for 20 seconds.

To shallow-fry: cover the bottom of a heavy-bottomed frying pan with 1 inch (2 cm) of cooking oil. When the oil is hot, fry one tortilla at a time for about 20 seconds. Remove from the oil and drain on absorbent kitchen paper until required.

To deep-fry: heat at least 4 inches (10 cm) of oil in a deep fryer, to a temperature of 400°F/200°C as for potato chips. Immerse the tortillas and fry for 1–1½ minutes. With practice you may fry four or five tortillas at once if they are whole. Remove from the oil when they are light golden, as they keep browning after they have been removed. Drain on absorbent kitchen towels and eat cold.

To fry Totopos (page 44), you may fry as many as your fryer will hold, but make sure to stir them so they fry evenly.

TORTILLAS DE HARINA DE TRIGO

(Wheat flour tortillas)　　　　Makes approx. 18 tortillas, 9 inches (24 cm) in diameter

1 tablespoon (15 ml spoon) salt

1 lb (450 g) plain flour

3 oz (75 g) lard or vegetable shortening

10 fl oz (275 ml) warm water (at body temperature)

Wheat flour tortillas are larger than corn tortillas and they come from northern Mexico, where maize does not grow so easily. They are made with animal fat, salt and plain white flour. Cooked on a hot griddle, they must be very pliable and soft for storage. For most purposes flour tortillas can be used in place of corn tortillas, and many people prefer them. They should be treated in the same manner and never eaten cold. To store flour tortillas you have to place waxed paper between them, as they tend to stick together, especially when frozen. They defrost easily if left at room temperature for 30 minutes.

Heat up a heavy-bottomed frying pan (without greasing it) on moderate heat until a drop of water in it sizzles. Sieve the salt and flour together, and blend in the fat as you would for ordinary pastry. Add warm water slowly – the amount may vary with the type of flour used, but only by a teaspoon (5 ml spoon) or two.

Knead the dough on a floured board with floured hands until it is no longer sticky, but is not hard. Keep the dough covered with a warm, damp cloth. Take approximately 1½ oz (45 g) dough at a time and knead, folding it back on itself to trap air for a few seconds (1). Now make it into a little ball and flatten it (2). Place the flattened ball on a floured board, and roll it out with a floured rolling pin until it is so thin that you can see the board through the pastry (3). Cut

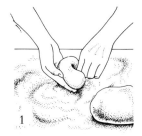

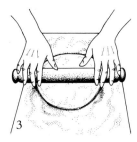

out the tortillas by placing a 9-inch (24 cm) plate on the thin dough and cutting around it (4).

Pick up each tortilla, lay it on your right hand and place it carefully on the moderately hot griddle or pan, making sure it is flat and has no folds. As it cooks it will thicken slightly and small bubbles will appear. Cook for about 40 seconds on one side and then turn it and cook it for about 30 seconds on the other side. When cooked it should feel heavy and floppy, soft and pliable.

Stack the cooked tortillas together, wrapped in a clean tea-towel. Always eat them hot except when they have been fried, when they can be eaten cold if consumed within 4 hours. Flour tortillas are reheated in the same way as corn tortillas.

Tortillas de Harina de Trigo; Tortillas de Maiz

FRIJOLES

(Beans)   Makes approx. 2 pints (1.2 litres)

*1 lb (450 g) dried red
kidney, black or pinto beans*

*2 cloves of garlic, skewered
on a cocktail stick*

*2 teaspoons (2 × 5 ml
spoon) salt*

*2 teaspoons (2 × 5 ml
spoon) sugar*

*2 tablespoons (2 × 15 ml
spoon) cooking oil*

*½ medium-size onion,
chopped finely*

2 whole green chillies

Oven temperature:
Gas Mark 4/350°F/180°C

*Beans are a staple in the Mexican diet, and so never
hesitate to serve them as an accompaniment to
Mexican dishes, whatever your choice of menu. The
preparation starts two days before because they need to
soak overnight and because they taste better the day
after they are cooked. Since beans take a long time to
cook, I suggest you cook 1 lb (450 g) at a time and
freeze what you do not need.*

Examine the beans carefully for small stones,
which are sometimes mixed in and are real
tooth-breakers. Wash the beans in a strainer
under the tap until the water is clear. Soak in
water overnight, allowing about 5 inches (12
cm) of water above the level of the beans. (If you
have forgotten to soak the beans overnight, you
can put them in cold water, bring them to the
boil and boil for 15 minutes and then soak them
for just an hour.)

When ready to cook, add the garlic and boil
the beans at a rolling boil for up to 3 hours or
until they feel very soft between the fingers.
They need to be topped up with boiling water
frequently. Discard the garlic cloves, then add
the salt and sugar and simmer gently for 10
minutes.

In the meantime, heat the cooking oil and
sauté the onion until golden. Add to the beans,
with the oil. Add the chillies, simmer for
another 15 minutes and then discard the chillies.
If the liquid looks very watery, mash some beans
against the side of the pot to thicken the mixture
and simmer for a little longer.

Cool and refrigerate until required (for up to 8
days). To serve, preheat the oven; then place the
beans in a casserole and cover. Cook for about
30 minutes. To freeze, cool and pack in airtight
containers. To serve, thaw at room temperature
for about 2 hours and heat as above or re-fry (see
next recipe).

FRIJOLES REFRITOS

(Re-fried beans)   Makes approx. 1¼ lb (550 g); serves 4

2 tablespoons (2 × 15 ml spoon) cooking oil

½ onion, half sliced thickly and the other half chopped finely for garnish

1 pint (600 ml) cooked beans (half the preceding Frijoles recipe)

In Mexico beans are served at each meal and are re-fried at each serving. In fact, re-fried beans become tastier with each frying as the flavour is intensified. Do make sure, however, that the other dishes in your menu are not too dry, as re-fried beans are about the consistency of mashed potatoes. This dish is a versatile filling or accompaniment and is suggested for use in many other recipes in this book.

Heat the oil in a large heavy frying pan, and fry the thick slices of onion in it until dark brown. Discard the onion and add the beans, mashing them with a potato masher whilst they fry.

Keep stirring the beans as they tend to stick to the bottom and sides of the pan and could burn. If they do stick, make a hole in the centre and add 1 tablespoon (15 ml spoon) of oil at a time as required.

When the beans are the consistency of thick porridge, they are good for spreading over tortillas or bread. If you like them really dry, keep stirring until you can toss them in the air in the frying pan as you would a pancake.

If serving as an accompaniment, garnish with the reserved onion and serve hot with Totopos (page 44).

If you need to re-fry the beans yet again, use a little water to soften them first.

SALSA DE JITOMATE

(Cooked tomato sauce)   Makes 1½ pints (900 ml)

1 onion, chopped finely

2 tablespoons (2 × 15 ml spoon) cooking oil

2 × 1 lb 3 oz (539 g) can of tomatoes

2 tablespoons (2 × 15 ml spoon) tomato purée (optional)

2 whole green chillies

1 chicken stock cube

a pinch of ground black pepper

a pinch of sugar

This is a handy basic sauce which is very simple but tasty. It is present in most Mexican dishes and excellent to cook in bulk, as it freezes very well. It is used in a variety of main course dishes and snacks, and can even be used with spaghetti bolognese, lasagne and pizza. In Mexico fresh tomatoes would be charred, peeled and mashed, but canned peeled tomatoes are much more economical in Britain, and the flavour is just as good.

Sauté the onion in the hot oil. Liquidise the tomatoes and their juice in a blender and add to the onion, along with the rest of the ingredients. Simmer gently for 15 minutes or until the chillies are soft.

   If you do not want your sauce hot, remember to remove the chillies before storing. If you like it hot, slice the chillies, tasting as you go to control the amount of 'sting'.

Below: Picadillo, Chorizo; Opposite: Guacamole, Salcita de Jitomate, Frijoles Refritos, Frijoles, Salsa de Jitomate

SALCITA DE JITOMATE

(Raw tomato sauce)   Makes approx. 1 pint (600 ml)

8 ripe, firm tomatoes, chopped finely

15 sprigs of fresh coriander, chopped finely

1 onion, chopped finely

4 green chillies, chopped very finely (optional)

juice of 1 lime or lemon

1 teaspoon (5 ml spoon) salt

½ teaspoon (2.5 ml spoon) ground black pepper

This is an excellent sauce to use as filling for soft warm tortillas. You can also use it as a topping for Taco Shells (page 67) or as a colourful side dish with a meal. This sauce does not keep, however, either frozen or refrigerated; it must be eaten within 4 hours of preparation.

Simply mix all the ingredients together thoroughly, 20 minutes before eating if possible. Serve cold.

GUACAMOLE

(Avocado dip)   Makes approx. 1 pint (600 ml)

4 ripe, firm tomatoes, chopped finely

10 sprigs of fresh coriander, chopped finely

½ onion, chopped finely

2 green chillies, chopped very finely (optional)

juice of 1 lime or lemon

1 teaspoon (5 ml spoon) salt

½ teaspoon (2.5 ml spoon) ground black pepper

1 large, ripe avocado

Guacamole is one of the most famous of Mexican dishes. Mole is the Nahuatl word for sauce and guaca stands for the shape of the avocado. Guacamole makes a delicious hors d'oeuvre or side dish, as well as an ingredient in many of the other recipes.

Mix the tomatoes, coriander, onion, chillies, half the lime or lemon juice, salt and pepper together not more than half an hour ahead.

Half an hour later, cut the avocado in half and spoon out the flesh, scraping the skin thoroughly to get the strong green colour. Mash it with a fork and mix into the tomato mixture.

To help stop the mixture from going brown, immerse the avocado stone in it. Smooth the surface and pour the remaining lime or lemon juice all over; then cover with cling film.

Just before serving, remove the cling film, pour off the extra lime or lemon juice and stir the mixture. If using as a starter, serve in a bowl surrounded by Totopos (page 44); the recipe will serve six in this way.

PICADILLO

(Savoury minced meat filling)   Makes approx. 1½ lb (675 g); serves 8

Ingredients
8 oz (225 g) minced beef
8 oz (225 g) minced pork
1 tablespoon (15 ml spoon) malt vinegar
¼ teaspoon (1.25 ml spoon) salt
a pinch of ground black pepper
a pinch of sugar
2 tablespoons (2 × 15 ml spoon) cooking oil
1 onion, chopped finely
1 clove of garlic, chopped finely
1 green pepper, chopped
2 green chillies, chopped finely (optional)
1 chicken stock cube
1 potato, cooked and diced
18 stuffed olives
2 tablespoons (2 × 15 ml spoon) flaked almonds
2 tablespoons (2 × 15 ml spoon) raisins
3 tablespoons (3 × 15 ml spoon) tomato purée
½ pint (300 ml) water

Picadillo is the common name for minced meat. It is often served with white rice but is also a very versatile filling for Empanadas (page 70), Tacos (page 67) and Chiles Rellenos (page 62).

Season the meats with the vinegar, salt and black pepper and add the pinch of sugar.

Heat the oil in a heavy frying pan and sauté the onion, garlic, pepper and chillies. Add the meats and fry, stirring frequently, for about 10–15 minutes until the mixture starts to brown. Discard the surplus oil, taking care not to pour away the meat juices.

Add all other ingredients and simmer gently for about 15 minutes, stirring occasionally until the mixture starts to dry. Eat hot, unless using as a filling in Empanadas, when it should be allowed to cool first. Picadillo can be refrigerated or frozen.

CHORIZO

(Spicy sausage)   Makes approx. 12 oz (350 g)

8 oz (225 g) pork, minced coarsely
3 oz (75 g) pork fat, minced
3 tablespoons (3 × 15 ml spoon) malt vinegar
½ teaspoon (2.5 ml spoon) salt
½ teaspoon (2.5 ml spoon) ground black pepper
2 cloves of garlic, crushed
2 teaspoons (2 × 5 ml spoon) cayenne pepper
1 tablespoon (15 ml spoon) paprika
1 teaspoon (5 ml spoon) coriander seeds
½ teaspoon (2.5 ml spoon) powdered cinnamon
½ teaspoon (2.5 ml) spoon oregano
½ teaspoon (2.5 ml spoon) marjoram
a pinch of grated nutmeg
a pinch of ground cloves

A convenient standby if you want to make meat go a long way and have a spicy flavour in your dish. It keeps best when well refrigerated and stirred every day, but eat within 10 days. If you prefer you could ask your butcher to put it into sausage casings and then keep it hanging in a cool place so that it is well aired all the time.

Mix all the ingredients together thoroughly. Place in a refrigerator in a non-metal bowl and marinate overnight. At this stage you may start eating it, if desired. Keep it uncovered in the fridge and stir daily. To cook, stir the desired amount into a little hot oil and fry for 5–7 minutes until crisp and crumbled. Use as a garnish for antojitos (light meals) or as a flavouring for other foods.

FRIJOLES DE LATA

(Tinned beans)   Makes approx. 3½ lb (1.6 kg)

2 tablespoons (2 × 15 ml spoon) cooking oil
2 cloves of garlic, crushed
1 onion, chopped finely
4 × 14 oz (400 g) cans of red kidney beans
2 green chillies, chopped

Cooked canned beans can be found on most supermarket shelves and can cut the preparation time of Mexican dishes drastically. Follow these instructions to produce a true Mexican flavour.

Heat the oil in a frying pan and fry the garlic until black. Discard the clove and add the onion, fry for 3 minutes and then add the beans and their

½ teaspoon (2.5 ml spoon)
salt

liquid and the remaining ingredients. Simmer over a medium heat until the liquid is absorbed and the consistency of the beans is that of thick porridge, about an hour. If you wish, you can mash the beans for re-fried beans.

CALDO DE POLLO

(Mexican-style chicken stock)   Makes 2 pints (1.2 litres)

a 3 lb (1.3 kg) fresh chicken, preferably with the giblets

1 scant teaspoon (5 ml spoon) salt

¼ teaspoon (1.25 ml spoon) ground black pepper

3 tablespoons (3 × 15 ml spoon) malt vinegar

4 pints (2.25 litres) water

1 chicken stock cube

2 sticks of celery, chopped

2 medium-size carrots, chopped

3 cabbage leaves, shredded

6 sprigs of fresh coriander or parsley

3 cloves of garlic

3 medium-size onions, chopped

Caldo de Pollo is a must for Mexican soups. It is economical because it utilises the goodness in the carcass, leaving the flesh for use in other dishes. The recipe is also suitable for beef or lamb bones. This stock can be served as consommé – garnish with fresh lime. It will then serve six.

Wash the chicken well, inside and out. Remove the 'parson's nose' and any yellow skin on the giblets.

Put the chicken in a large saucepan with all the other ingredients. Cover and simmer at boiling point for 1 hour. Skim off any foam that comes to the surface. Test the chicken for readiness by pricking the drumstick. If only white liquid comes out and the leg feels loose, the chicken is ready.

Remove the chicken, strain the vegetables and taste the stock; if the flavour is weak, add one more stock cube and boil for a further 5 minutes. Skim off all the grease. This is done more successfully after the stock has been refrigerated for 2 hours.

The cold chicken meat can be used in other dishes, such as Tostadas (page 32), Budin Azteca (page 66) or Tacos (page 67).

ANTOJITOS
(Light meals)

Antojitos literally means 'little whims', i.e. 'what you fancy'. They are so irresistible that whether you are hungry or not you're bound to develop an appetite at whatever time of the day or night you smell these freshly cooked savouries. They are sold in markets and on street corners and are almost the Mexican equivalent of fish and chips, but in a hundred different varieties.

For family cooking, antojitos are outstanding. They are quick to prepare, satisfying and a great way to use leftovers. Antojitos are usually accompanied by Guacamole, Salcita de Jitomate (see previous section) or soured cream, with chopped lettuce and finely chopped raw onion for garnish. Often they are used as bocadillos (hors d'oeuvres) before a meal. For cocktail parties, which are now creeping into the Mexican way of life, many of the traditional antojitos are made bite-size.

MOYETES

(Crusty rolls spread with beans)　　　　　　　　　　　　Serves 4

Basic recipe: Frijoles Refritos (page 19)

4 crusty rolls	Moyetes are often served for breakfast and are very popular instead of bread and butter as an accompaniment to egg dishes.
1 oz (25 g) butter	
8 oz (225 g) Frijoles Refritos	
2 oz (50 g) mild Cheddar cheese, grated	Cut each roll in half and remove some of the soft inside. Spread with butter and some of the re-fried beans and sprinkle them with the cheese and raw onion. Bake for 15–20 minutes. Eat hot.
¼ onion, chopped finely	
Oven temperature: Gas Mark 2/300°F/150°C	

HUEVOS RANCHEROS

(Ranch-style eggs)　　　　　　　　　　　　　　　　　　Serves 4

Basic recipes: Tortillas (pages 11–16); Frijoles Refritos (page 19); Salsa de Jitomate (page 20)

16 corn tortillas or 8 wheat flour tortillas	Huevos Rancheros are a good example of a Mexican almuerzo ('brunch') dish and are suitable for a light lunch or supper.
oil for deep frying	
8 oz (225 g) Frijoles Refritos	Deep-fry the tortillas in very hot oil. If they puff up as they fry, press them flat with a kitchen spoon. Drain on absorbent kitchen paper and keep warm.
8 eggs	
1 pint (600 ml) Salsa de Jitomate	Warm the beans and spread them over the fried tortillas. Fry the eggs and place them on top of the beans, then spoon the hot tomato sauce over them.

BURRITOS

(Wheat flour tortillas with a filling)   Serves 6–8

Basic recipes: Tortillas (pages 11–16); Frijoles Refritos (page 19);
Guacamole (page 22) or Salcita de Jitomate (page 20)

6–8 wheat flour tortillas

1 tablespoon (15 ml spoon) cooking oil

1 onion, sliced

1¼ lb (550 g) Frijoles Refritos

1 small lettuce, shredded finely

3 ripe tomatoes, sliced thinly

6 spring onions, chopped finely

8 oz (225 g) mild Cheddar cheese, grated finely

12 tablespoons (12 × 15 ml spoon) Guacamole or Salcita

Oven temperatures:
Gas Mark 2/300°F/150°C
Gas Mark 4/350°F/180°C

This dish, which has been christened by the Americans and means literally 'little donkeys', is deservedly popular. The filling, like that for corn tortillas, may be just about any meat or vegetable, egg or beans. Try the following recipe first, then improvise with whatever filling you fancy. Fresh chopped onions and lettuce plus a sauce such as Guacamole (page 22) will go well with any filling.

Heat the tortillas wrapped in aluminium foil in the oven, at the lower temperature, for 10 minutes just to make them pliable.

Heat the oil and sauté the onion. Then add the beans and stir for about 5 minutes until they are nice and hot.

Put 2 tablespoons (2 × 15 ml spoon) in the centre of each tortilla, sprinkle with the lettuce and add tomato slices, spring onions and cheese. Fold it like a parcel and secure with one or more cocktail sticks.

Put the Burritos in an ovenproof dish, cover them with aluminium foil very securely and heat them for 20 minutes in the oven, at the higher temperature. Before serving lace with the Guacamole or Salcita.

Burritos

TORTAS

(Mexican sandwiches)   Serves 4

Basic recipes: Frijoles Refritos (page 19); Chiles en Vinagre (see following recipe), optional

Ingredients
1 french stick (baguette size) cut into four, or 4 large crusty rolls
8 oz (225 g) Frijoles Refritos
4 slices of processed cheese, ham, cooked chicken or cold pork
½ lettuce, shredded finely
½ onion, sliced finely in rings
2 tomatoes, sliced finely
1 avocado, sliced
4 tablespoons (4 × 15 ml spoon) soured cream
Chiles en Vinagre, optional

Tortas are the Mexican answer to sandwiches, but they are much more elaborate and one is usually enough for a light lunch. The most popular Mexican Tortas are made in torterias, *a type of take-away shop. The bread used is called* telera, *which is similar to a large crusty bun or a piece of a crusty french stick. In Mexico the bread is usually baked before each meal, but you can simply wrap it in foil and warm it in a moderate oven for about 15 minutes. The fillings can be as varied as you like, although the following mixture is delicious.*

Cut the piece of bread or each roll in half and remove the centre. Spread the bottom with the warm re-fried beans and then top with a slice of the cheese or meat, some lettuce, some onion rings and tomato slices, a slice or two of avocado and a tablespoon (15 ml spoon) of soured cream. Top with Chiles en Vinagre, if desired, and replace the hollowed-out top piece of bread.

CHILES EN VINAGRE

(Pickled peppers)   Makes 2 pints (1.2 litres)

6 tablespoons (6 × 15 ml
spoon) cooking oil

12 green chillies, sliced
thinly

4 large carrots, peeled and
sliced thinly in rounds

2 large onions, sliced thinly

1 red pepper, sliced thinly

1 pint (600 ml) distilled
malt vinegar

2 cloves of garlic, chopped
finely

¼ teaspoon (1.25 ml
spoon) oregano

¼ teaspoon (1.25 ml
spoon) marjoram

¼ teaspoon (1.25 ml
spoon) thyme

1 teaspoon (5 ml spoon) salt

½ teaspoon (2.5 ml spoon)
ground black pepper

1 tablespoon (15 ml spoon)
granulated sugar

*These pickles go particularly well with cheese and are
also good in sandwiches, especially the Tortas in the
preceding recipe and the Tostadas in the next recipe.
They will keep very well in the refrigerator but
remember to try only a little at a time!*

Avoid handling the chillies with your bare
hands, or you'll have 'hot' fingers for days –
especially noticeable when you rub your nose,
eyes or skin! Wear kitchen gloves or at least
handle the chillies with respect; use a knife and
fork, and cut them over kitchen paper towels
which you discard afterwards.

Heat the oil in a large saucepan and toss the
chillies, carrots, onions and red pepper for 2
minutes each, removing them from the heat and
setting them aside in a bowl until they are all
done. Slowly add the vinegar, herbs, seasoning
and sugar to the oil and boil until the liquid is
reduced by one-third. Pour the boiling liquid
over the vegetables and allow to cool uncovered.
When cold, transfer to clean jars and seal.
Refrigerate once a jar is opened.

TOSTADAS

(Fried crisp corn tortillas piled with salad)   Makes 8

Basic recipes: Tortillas (pages 11–16); Frijoles Refritos (page 19);
Chiles en Vinagre (see preceding recipe)

8 corn tortillas

oil for deep frying

8 oz (225 g) Frijoles
Refritos

½ lettuce, shredded finely

2 cooked chicken breasts,
shredded finely

4 tomatoes, sliced finely

½ onion, sliced in rings

1 avocado, sliced

8 tablespoons (8 × 15 ml
spoon) soured cream

2 oz (50 g) mild Cheddar
cheese, grated

Chiles en Vinagre

salt and black pepper

Tostadas are very popular throughout Mexico, and the filling varies according to the area: it can be crab, chicken, beef, pork, turkey or just salad. Whatever the filling, it is very colourful and is piled up until it looks like a little pyramid – almost impossible to eat, but Mexicans love pyramids, so why not join them!

Deep-fry the tortillas in the oil and warm the re-fried beans. Spread each tortilla with the warm beans and then lay on some of the lettuce, chicken, tomato, onion and avocado slices.

Spoon 1 tablespoon (15 ml spoon) of the soured cream over each Tostada. Sprinkle with some cheese and add pickled peppers and a pinch of salt and black pepper. Eat immediately.

To eat, lift the whole Tostada with your hand, making sure you do not tilt it. Take a small bite at a time so you don't crack it and cause it all to drop on to your plate! You might also end up with a never-ending mouthful, if you attempt big bites. Serve one per person as a snack or two or more for a light meal.

Tortas; Tostadas; Chiles en Vinagre

HUEVOS CON TORTILLA

(Tortilla omelette) Serves 4

Basic recipes: Tortillas (pages 11–16); Salsa de Jitomate (page 20)

3 fried tortillas, quartered into bite-size pieces

4 tablespoons (4 × 15 ml spoon) cooking oil, plus more for deep frying

½ onion, chopped

4 large eggs (size 2), lightly beaten and mixed with 1 teaspoon (5 ml spoon) water

6 sprigs of parsley, chopped finely

2 green chillies (optional)

a pinch of salt

a pinch of ground black pepper

6 tablespoons (6 × 15 ml spoon) Salsa de Jitomate

A quick and tasty way of eating eggs, this would make a popular light supper or brunch.

Fry the tortilla pieces in a deep fat fryer until golden brown, about 3 minutes.

Heat the 4 tablespoons (4 × 15 ml spoon) oil in a frying pan, and sauté the onion. Add the beaten egg, parsley, chillies if used, tortilla pieces, salt and pepper. Stir slowly, moving the egg mixture to one side and tilting the frying pan to ensure that all the egg gets cooked.

In order to cook the egg mixture on the other side, transfer it from the frying pan on to a dinner plate. Now place the frying pan upside-down over the plate. Holding both the plate and the frying pan with oven gloves, turn them over so that the plate is uppermost. Remove the plate and return the frying pan to the heat for 1 more minute. (All this extra trouble should produce a rounded omelette about 1 inch/2.5 cm thick.) Spread the tomato sauce over it and serve hot, accompanied by Frijoles Refritos (page 19).

HUEVOS REVUELTOS CON CHORIZO

(Scrambled eggs with spicy sausage)   Serves 4

Basic recipe: Chorizo (page 24), optional

1 tablespoon (15 ml spoon)
cooking oil

6 oz (175 g) Chorizo,
bought or home-made

2 ripe firm tomatoes,
quartered

¼ onion, chopped finely

¼ teaspoon (1.25 ml
spoon) salt

¼ teaspoon (1.25 ml
spoon) ground black pepper

1 green chilli, sliced

1 tablespoon (15 ml spoon)
cold water

6 eggs, well beaten

This is my favourite way of eating eggs for breakfast,
but it will also make a good lunch accompanied by rice.
I particularly like it on crispy, warm and buttered
french bread. It goes down well with the family, too.
As an alternative, re-fry this mixture with beans,
omitting the eggs.

Heat the oil in a frying pan and fry the Chorizo
for about 5 minutes until crispy, stirring
frequently. Add the tomatoes, onion, salt,
pepper and chilli, and cook for another 3
minutes, tossing carefully so that the tomato
does not squash. Add the water to the beaten
eggs and pour over the tomato and Chorizo
mixture. Stir occasionally to prevent the egg
from burning. Slide on to a warm dish and eat
immediately.

PAPAS CON CHORIZO

(Fried potatoes with spicy sausage)   Serves 4

Basic recipe: Chorizo (page 24), optional

1 teaspoon (5 ml spoon)
cooking oil

6 oz (175 g) Chorizo,
bought or home-made

½ onion, chopped finely

1 green chilli, chopped
finely (optional)

1 lb (450 g) potatoes, boiled
and mashed

2 oz (50 g) Cheddar cheese,
grated

salt and ground black pepper

A very popular way of using leftover mashed or
cooked potato, but well worth the trouble of cooking
the potatoes especially.

Heat the oil and sauté the Chorizo and onion for
about 3 minutes, then add the chilli, if used.
When the Chorizo is crispy, add the mashed
potatoes and continue frying until they start
turning golden. Add salt and black pepper,
sprinkle with the cheese and place under a grill
just until the cheese melts.

ENFRIJOLADAS

(Fried tortillas with beans and sauce)   Serves 4

Basic recipes: Tortillas (pages 11–16); Frijoles Refritos (page 19);
Salsa de Jitomate (page 20); Chorizo (page 24), optional

4 fl oz (110 ml) cooking oil	*Another antojito that is easy and quick to prepare.*
8 corn tortillas or 4 wheat flour tortillas	*This is a combination of tortillas, beans and sauce, garnished with a little Spanish chorizo sausage*
1¼ lb (550 g) Frijoles Refritos	*(available from delicatessen counters or home-made). The quantities below are enough for a light lunch or supper.*
½ pint (300 ml) Salsa de Jitomate	

4 oz (100 g) crumbly white cheese, such as Wensleydale

1 onion, chopped finely

8 oz (225 g) Chorizo, crumbled, fried and drained

2 green chillies, chopped finely

Heat the oil in a frying pan and toss each tortilla in it for 1 minute, turning once and removing from the oil when just light brown. Drain the tortillas on absorbent paper and keep them warm. Spread each tortilla with the hot re-fried beans and 2 tablespoons (2 × 15 ml spoon) of the cooked tomato sauce and then sprinkle it with some of the cheese, onion, Chorizo and chillies. Serve immediately.

CHILAQUILES

(Crispy fried corn tortillas in tomato sauce)   Serves 4

Basic recipes: Tortillas (pages 11–16); Salsa de Jitomate (page 20)

oil for deep frying

12 corn tortillas, cut into 8 pieces each

1 pint (600 ml) Salsa de Jitomate

1 medium-size onion, chopped finely

Optional extras:

2 green chillies, chopped finely

4 tablespoons (4 × 15 ml spoon) soured cream

2 oz (50 g) Wensleydale cheese, crumbled

These go very well with Frijoles Refritos (page 19) and are a traditional breakfast dish which is good enough for lunch or light supper. Excellent in an emergency if you have some tortillas in the freezer.

Heat the oil to 400°F/200°C and fry the tortillas until they start changing colour. Drain them and keep them warm. Bring the sauce to the boil, drop the tortilla chips into it and bring to the boil again. Transfer the mixture to a warm serving dish and garnish it with the chopped onion and the chillies if used. Add the soured cream and cheese before garnishing if you wish to turn it into a lunch or supper dish.

Enfrijoladas; Chilaquiles

QUESADILLAS

(Cheese-filled tortillas)   Serves 4

Basic recipe: Tortillas (pages 11–16)

8 corn tortillas or 4 wheat flour tortillas

4 oz (100 g) mild Cheddar cheese, grated

½ onion, sliced finely in rings

2 green chillies, cut in strips (optional)

Oven temperature:
Gas Mark 4/350°F/180°C (if reheating)

This is a popular snack which can be glorified and turned into a light lunch by serving it hot with re-fried beans and a sauce. It is extremely palatable to British people, who already have such a strong liking for cheese.

Heat a griddle or heavy frying pan until it sizzles when a few drops of water are sprinkled on it. Lay a tortilla on the hot surface and arrange about 1 oz (25 g) of the grated cheese over it to cover, followed by one or two onion rings and some chilli strips if desired. Now place another tortilla on top, and leave on a medium heat for 1½ minutes.

When the cheese starts to melt, carefully turn the Quesadilla over and leave it for one more minute. When the cheese is nicely melted, remove it from the heat and serve immediately.

If you wish to prepare a large number at once, make parcels of about 12 tortillas wrapped together in aluminium foil. Place one foil parcel at a time in a double boiler and steam for 15 minutes. Unwrap and spread each half of a tortilla with cheese, onion and chilli if used, fold in half whilst still hot and secure with a cocktail stick.

When all the tortillas have been steamed and filled, place them on a baking tray, wrap in aluminium foil and leave until required. To reheat them, first preheat the oven and then place them, still well wrapped, in the oven for 15 minutes, until the cheese melts. Serve immediately.

Suggested accompaniments are Frijoles Refritos (page 19) and either Salcita de Jitomate or Guacamole (page 22).

BOCADILLOS
Y ENTREMESES
(Hors d'oeuvres and starters)

Meals in Mexico are at no set time, so that
bocadillos are very necessary as well as popular,
especially for celebrations. You might be invited
at two o'clock for lunch and the meal may not
actually start until four o'clock. But the
bocadillos, accompanied by tequila, mezcal or
beer will, in fact, provide delicious hors
d'oeuvres before the meal properly begins.

The influence of Spain and France in Mexican
cuisine is very evident and the delightful mixture
that results is pleasing to both eye and palate.
Olives are often offered by themselves, and
anchovies and smoked oysters on crackers are
also popular, as are peanuts tossed in a healthy
helping of cayenne pepper. I have included in
this section some recipes for the most popular
bocadillos, bearing in mind the availability of
ingredients in Britain.

Sopa, soup, is a dish acquired from colonial
times, and despite the heat in the middle of the
day no meal is complete without it. It is served
hot throughout the year. A good *caldo*, or stock,
is of utmost importance, and the basic Mexican
stock (page 25) is well worth making in quantity
to give extra flavour to the soup recipes on the
following pages. Ingredients such as beans,
avocados, pumpkin blossoms, stale tortillas and
fresh and dried chillies provide a great diversity
of flavours.

More unusual is the second soup, called *sopa
seca*, 'dry soup', which is also generally served
before the meat course. These 'soups' usually
consist of rice or pasta cooked in tomato sauce
and stock (which is absorbed in the cooking) and
finally sprinkled with cheese.

CEBICHE

(Marinated fish)   Serves 8 as a starter or 4 as a lunch

Basic recipe: Salcita de Jitomate (page 22)

1 lb (450 g) cod or haddock fillets, skinned

1 medium-size onion, sliced finely

juice of 1 orange

juice of 5 limes or lemons

4 tablespoons (4 × 15 ml spoon) olive oil

3 tablespoons (3 × 15 ml spoon) tomato ketchup

1 teaspoon (5 ml spoon) Worcestershire sauce

½ teaspoon (2.5 ml spoon) oregano

½ teaspoon (2.5 ml spoon) salt

¼ teaspoon (1.25 ml spoon) ground black pepper

½ pint (300 ml) Salcita de Jitomate

To garnish:

avocado slices (optional)

Cebiche is the traditional dish of the coastal towns, where it takes many different guises, the ingredients being as varied as the people that prepare it. Red snapper is the most popular fish used, but cod and haddock can be used instead. Whatever your views on eating raw fish, do try it!

Inspect the fish carefully for bones and remove them. Cut the fillets into small, bite-size pieces and place in a bowl with the sliced onion and the fresh orange and lime or lemon juice, taking care that all the fish is well covered. Cover and leave in the refrigerator to marinate overnight, or for at least 3 hours.

An hour before serving, add the remaining ingredients, stir and then leave to marinate until required. The fish will have 'cooked' in the acidic fruit juice and should be white, not transparent. Serve cold, garnished if desired with avocado slices and accompanied by water biscuits.

Cebiche; Salpicón de Hongos; Jaiba al Horno

JAIBA AL HORNO

(Baked crab)   Serves 4

2 oz (50 g) butter or
margarine

1 medium-size onion,
chopped finely

5 sprigs of fresh parsley,
chopped finely

6 oz (175 g) white crab
meat, fresh, canned or
frozen

2 dashes of Tabasco sauce

1/4 teaspoon (1.25 ml
spoon) Worcestershire sauce

1/2 chicken stock cube

a pinch of ground black
pepper

3 tablespoons (3 × 15 ml
spoon) tomato purée

2 tablespoons (2 × 15 ml
spoon) fine breadcrumbs

To garnish:

4 slices of lemon

Oven temperature:
Gas Mark 4/350°F/180°C

*This dish is excellent with either fresh or canned crab.
If you use whole crabs, scrub and save the crab shells,
as they can be used to bake the crab in.*

*In Mexico City it is possible to go to the fish market
and buy live crabs. In fact the market proudly
proclaims in huge letters 'The fish that you buy here
today slept in the sea last night.' The variety of fish
and seafood available is incredible.*

Heat the oven. Melt the butter or margarine in a
heavy frying pan and sauté the onion and parsley
for 2 minutes. Drain the crab meat well and add
it to the pan, along with all the other ingredients
except for the breadcrumbs and lemon. Fry over
a moderate heat, stirring frequently, until the
mixture starts to dry.

Spoon on to well-buttered scallop or crab
shells and bake in the oven. After 15 minutes
sprinkle the breadcrumbs on top and return to
the oven; when the breadcrumbs are lightly
browned it is ready. Serve hot, garnished with
the lemon slices.

SALPICÓN DE HONGOS

(Marinated mushrooms)   Serves 4

2 tablespoons (2 × 15 ml
spoon) cooking oil

1 clove of garlic

8 oz (225 g) mushrooms,
sliced coarsely

1 medium-size onion, sliced

1 carrot, grated finely

2 sticks of celery, sliced
crossways

1 green pepper, sliced

1 chilli, chopped finely

juice of ½ lime or lemon

1 chicken stock cube or a
pinch of salt (optional)

a pinch of sugar

a pinch of ground black
pepper

6 sprigs of fresh coriander,
chopped finely

4 oz (100 g) full fat soft
cheese (optional)

*A quick and easy dish to be used as a cold starter or as a
hot filling for soft, warm tortillas. Ideal for
vegetarians.*

Heat the oil in a heavy skillet and sauté the garlic
clove until dark golden. Discard the garlic clove,
then sauté the mushrooms, onion, carrot,
celery, pepper and chilli for 5 minutes. Add the
lime or lemon juice, crumbled stock cube,
sugar, black pepper and coriander. Cover and
simmer for a further 5 minutes. Serve cold.

To serve hot, add the soft cheese and use as
filling for tortillas.

TOTOPOS

(Tortilla chips)   Serves 4

Basic recipe: Tortillas (pages 11–16)

6–8 tortillas	*Everyone loves tortilla chips, and they are an*
oil for deep frying	*excellent alternative to crisps. You can make them*
2 teaspoons (2 × 5 ml spoon) salt	*well in advance since they will keep in an airtight container for up to a week.*

4 tablespoons (4 × 15 ml spoon) parmesan cheese (optional)

½ teaspoon (2.5 ml spoon) cayenne pepper (optional)

Cut the tortillas into quarters and then cut each quarter in half to form eight triangles (see diagram). Alternatively, corn tortillas can be cut into strips, 2 × ½-inch (4 × 1 cm), but this is not advisable for wheat flour tortillas, which break too easily.

Heat the oil to the same temperature as for frying chips, about 400°F/200°C. Fry the pieces until they are light brown, stirring them occasionally and making sure all the tortillas brown evenly. Drain them on absorbent paper and toss with the salt and parmesan and/or cayenne if required. Serve cold, alone or with a dip such as Guacamole (page 22) or Frijoles con Queso (page 50). These chips also make a good garnish for Frijoles Refritos (page 19).

CACAHUATES ENCHILADOS

(Peppered peanuts)   Serves 4

7 oz (200 g) packet of roasted peanuts

1 teaspoon (5 ml spoon) cayenne pepper

Peanuts are eaten in Mexico in many different ways: plain, roasted, peppered, sugared and also ground into sauces. This is one popular way of serving them.

Mix the peanuts thoroughly with the pepper. Offer in bowls with drinks.

Margarita cocktail (see page 92); Guacamole with Totopos; Cacahuates Enchilados

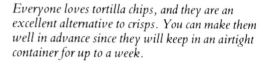

SOPA DE FRIJOL NEGRO

(Black bean soup)   Serves 8

Basic recipes: Frijoles (page 18); Caldo de Pollo (page 25), optional

2 tablespoons (2 × 15 ml spoon) cooking oil

1 pint (600 ml) Frijoles and their liquid, if any

2 tablespoons (2 × 15 ml spoon) tomato purée

½ onion

1 small clove of garlic

2 pints (1.2 litres) Caldo de Pollo or 3 chicken stock cubes dissolved in 2 pints (1.2 litres) boiling water

2 green chillies (optional)

8 sprigs of fresh coriander

a pinch of sugar

salt and black pepper

To garnish:

4 tablespoons (4 × 15 ml spoon) cooking oil

2 slices of stale white bread cut into ½-inch (1 cm) cubes

This is a delicious, hearty soup, as well as an excellent way of finishing leftover beans. It can actually be cooked with any type of bean, as the colour is unimportant and flavour varies only slightly. Black beans themselves, which are rich in iron and protein, have a slightly mushroomy flavour and lend the soup a distinctive colour. The crôutons are the perfect complement to this soup, but can also be used as a garnish for many other soups or even added to tossed green salads.

Heat the oil in a saucepan. Grind the beans, tomato purée, onion and garlic in a blender to a smooth paste, adding a little chicken stock if the mixture is too dry to blend.

Strain (or just pour) the mixture into the hot oil slowly to prevent it from splashing. Add the chicken stock, chillies, coriander, sugar and seasoning. Bring to the boil and simmer uncovered for 30 minutes, until thick. Discard the herbs and chillies; if you prefer it hot, chop the chillies finely and put them back in the soup.

In a frying pan, heat the remaining oil and fry the bread cubes until golden brown, stirring continually, and then drain them on absorbent kitchen paper. (Alternatively, you can bake them in the oven at Gas Mark 1/275°F/140°C, for 30 minutes, turning them occasionally.) Serve the soup in warm bowls garnished with the crôutons.

SOPA DE PORO Y PAPA

(Leek and potato soup) Serves 4

Basic recipe: Caldo de Pollo (page 25), optional

2 pints (1.2 litres) Caldo de Pollo or 3 chicken stock cubes dissolved in 2 pints (1.2 litres) boiling water

2 fresh leeks, sliced thinly

2 medium-size potatoes, peeled and cubed

2 tablespoons (2 × 15 ml spoon) fresh parsley or coriander, chopped finely

a pinch of sugar

5 fl oz (150 ml) carton of double cream (for cold soup only)

salt and ground black pepper

A simple and delicious soup. Eat it hot as it is, or cold by adding double cream and putting it in the blender.

Bring the stock to the boil. Add the leek and potato and simmer until tender. Add all the other ingredients and simmer for 20 minutes more. Serve hot.

For cold soup, allow to cool, and then add the double cream. Mix in a blender and serve garnished with more coriander or parsley.

SOPA DE AGUACATE

(Avocado soup) Serves 8

Basic recipe: Caldo de Pollo (page 25), optional

2 pints (1.2 litres) Caldo de Pollo or 3 chicken stock cubes dissolved in 2 pints (1.2 litres) boiling water

4 avocados, peeled

To garnish:

2 tablespoons (2 × 15 ml spoon) chopped fresh coriander

This soup is delicious at room temperature. It has a beautiful colour, which the flavour lives up to completely.

Reheat the stock if not using it freshly made and pour it into a blender. Add three of the avocados and blend at top speed for 30 seconds. Allow to cool to room temperature. Slice the remaining avocado and garnish the soup with the slices and with the coriander sprinkled over the top.

SOPA DE FIDEO

(Vermicelli soup)   Serves 4

Basic recipe: Caldo de Pollo (page 25), optional

6 tablespoons (6 × 15 ml spoon) cooking oil

4 oz (100 g) vermicelli

½ onion, quartered

1 clove of garlic, skewered on a cocktail stick

4 sprigs of parsley

2 whole chillies

2 pints (1.2 litres) Caldo de Pollo or 3 chicken stock cubes dissolved in 2 pints (1.2 litres) boiling water

3 tablespoons (3 × 15 ml spoon) tomato purée

To garnish:

2 oz (50 g) parmesan cheese

1 tablespoon (15 ml spoon) chopped parsley

This is an everyday soup in the Mexican home and is served 'dry', sprinkled with parmesan cheese and/or chopped fresh parsley. This dish improves if left overnight.

Heat the oil in a large frying pan and fry the vermicelli until it is golden brown – this happens very quickly. Remove the vermicelli with a slotted spoon and drain on absorbent paper.

Discard all but 2 tablespoons (2 × 15 ml spoon) of the oil and fry the onion and garlic until golden. Add the reserved vermicelli, parsley, chillies, stock and tomato purée and stir so that the purée is well mixed in.

Cover and simmer for 15 minutes; then uncover and cook for a further 30 minutes, stirring occasionally. When the mixture starts to dry out, it is ready to serve. Discard the onion, garlic, parsley and chillies and serve sprinkled with the parmesan cheese and chopped parsley or keep to reheat the next day.

Sopa de Poro y Papa; Sopa de Aguacate; Sopa de Fideo

FRIJOLES CON QUESO

(Bean and cheese dip)   Serves 6

Basic recipes: Frijoles Refritos (page 19); Salcita de Jitomate (page 22)

8 oz (225 g) Frijoles Refritos	*This is a good cocktail snack, served warm with Totopos (page 44).*
2 oz (50 g) mild Cheddar cheese, grated finely	Warm the re-fried beans if necessary; they should be the consistency of thick porridge. Add the grated cheese and stir for about 1 minute until the cheese melts. Remove from the heat and mix in the tomato sauce. Allow to cool to room temperature and serve with Totopos. (Stir just before serving if made in advance.)
½ pint (300 ml) Salcita de Jitomate	

FRIJOLES CON CREMA

(Bean dip)   Serves 8

Basic recipe: Frijoles Refritos (page 19)

4 ripe firm tomatoes, chopped finely	*This is a good stand-by if you are entertaining and your avocados have not ripened in time! But, you do need re-fried beans which must be already cooked. This dip will last longer than Guacamole and can be served at room temperature accompanied by Totopos (page 44).*
10 sprigs of fresh coriander, chopped finely	
½ onion, chopped finely	
2 green chillies, chopped very finely (optional)	Mix the tomatoes, coriander, onion, chillies, lime or lemon juice, salt and pepper together and set aside. Heat the oil, add the re-fried beans and stir them for 2 minutes until they are bubbling. Remove from the heat and add the cheeses, stirring constantly until they melt. Add the tomato mixture and single cream and serve at room temperature.
juice of 1 lime or lemon	
½ teaspoon (2.5 ml spoon) each of salt and black pepper	
2 teaspoons (2 × 5 ml spoon) cooking oil	
10 oz (275 g) Frijoles Refritos	
2 oz (50 g) Cheddar cheese, grated	
2 oz (50 g) cream cheese	
5 fl oz (150 ml) carton of single cream	

CAMARONES CON ALMENDRAS

(Prawns with almonds)   Serves 6

2 × 7 oz (200 g) can of
prawns, or 14 oz (400 g)
fresh cooked prawns

12 oz (350 g) can of
asparagus tips

a small jar of stuffed green
olives

2 tablespoons (2 × 15 ml
spoon) olive oil

4 spring onions, chopped
finely

2 tablespoons (2 × 15 ml
spoon) tomato purée

juice of 1 lemon

a pinch of sugar

½ teaspoon (2.5 ml spoon)
salt

½ teaspoon (2.5 ml spoon)
black pepper

3 tablespoons (3 × 15 ml
spoon) tomato ketchup

2 dashes of Worcestershire
sauce

2 dashes of Tabasco sauce

3 oz (75 g) flaked almonds

6 lettuce leaves, shredded

*This delicious starter can also make a light lunch.
Prepare it several hours ahead of time to give it a
chance to cool in the refrigerator.*

Drain the cans of prawns and asparagus tips,
reserving the liquid. Slice the olives. Heat the
olive oil and fry the spring onions for 3 minutes;
add the reserved liquid, tomato purée, lemon
juice, sugar, salt, black pepper, tomato ketchup,
Worcestershire sauce and Tabasco. Stir and
simmer gently for 5 minutes. Remove from the
heat, add the prawns, almonds, and olive slices,
reserving some for garnish. Mix and cool.

Before serving, divide the lettuce into six
portions, arrange the prawn mixture over them
and garnish with the reserved sliced olives and
asparagus tips.

NACHOS

(Crispy fried corn tortilla chips with melted cheese and chilli)   Serves 4

Basic recipes: Tortillas (pages 11–16); Chiles en Vinagre (page 31), optional

---

8 corn tortillas

oil for deep frying

1 tablespoon (15 ml spoon) Chiles en Vinagre, drained and chopped, or 3 green chillies, chopped finely

2 oz (50 g) mozzarella cheese, grated

2 oz (50 g) mature Cheddar cheese, grated

salt

Oven temperature: Gas Mark 2/300°F/150°C

Frijoles con Crema; Cocktail de Aguacate

This is a good appetiser to offer with cocktails. It is best eaten whilst still warm, and you are well advised to take time preparing each Nacho so the melted cheese does not bind them altogether in one mass!

Cut the tortillas into quarters. Heat the oil to the same temperature as for frying chips, about 400°F/200°C. Fry the pieces until they are light brown, stirring them occasionally and making sure all the tortillas brown evenly. Drain them on absorbent paper and toss with salt.

Heat the oven. Arrange the pieces on a baking sheet and sprinkle over the chopped Chiles en Vinagre or the chopped green chillies, then mix the two cheeses together and carefully sprinkle a little on to each piece of fried tortilla chip. Bake for 10 minutes.

Eat warm.

COCKTAIL DE AGUACATE

(Avocado cocktail)   Serves 8

8 fl oz (240 ml) tomato
ketchup

4 oz (100 g) cream cheese

juice of 1 lemon

½ teaspoon (2.5 ml spoon)
Worcestershire sauce

½ teaspoon (2.5 ml spoon)
Tabasco sauce

½ teaspoon (2.5 ml spoon)
ground black pepper

½ teaspoon (2.5 ml spoon)
salt

½ lettuce, shredded finely

4 ripe avocados

To garnish:

4 spring onions,
chopped finely

*Avocados are popular everywhere and in Mexico we
often have them in a cocktail instead of prawns, which
is good news for vegetarians. I quite enjoy this starter
served with salted cheese crackers.*

Mix together the ketchup, cream cheese, lemon,
Worcestershire sauce, Tabasco, black pepper
and salt, cover and stand for about 1 hour.

Just before serving, spoon the avocado flesh
out in large pieces. Divide the lettuce and place it
in the bottom of individual cocktail glasses. Lay
the avocado pieces on top and spoon over the
sauce and garnish with the chopped spring
onions.

Camarones con Almendras; Nachos

53

PLATOS FUERTES
(Main courses and accompaniments)

When the European olives, oil, garlic, coriander and onions were added to native corn, tomatoes, chillies and courgettes, the possible combinations for Mexican main meals with fish, meat and poultry became endless.

Mexico's coastline stretches over 6,000 miles and provides a great variety of shellfish as well as fresh fish. The cooking of all these has evolved from the simple steaming in *maguey* (agave) leaves to frying, grilling and stewing. It is said that Emperor Moctezuma ate fresh fish every day – it was delivered by relays of barefoot runners from the Gulf of Mexico to Tenochtitlan, the Aztec capital.

The turkey was found domesticated in Mexico in the sixteenth century. Chicken, introduced by Spain into the Americas, has for economic reasons established itself well in the Mexican cuisine, but the most traditional dish is still made with turkey.

Pork, beef, lamb and goat were all unknown to the Indians until the Spaniards arrived. Pork in particular became very popular, as it yielded fat for cooking – the indigenous diet had been practically fatless. The cheaper cuts of beef are often tough, hence its preparation in the form of stews and minced or shredded beef. Lamb is only popular in the form of *barbacoa*. This involves a primitive way of cooking the complete animal in a hole in the ground.

Mexico is a vegetarian's paradise, since apart from most of the European vegetables, which can be found all year round, there is a wealth of regional seasonal ones, which cooked in their traditional manner often become succulent main courses.

BUDIN AZTECA

(Chicken tortilla casserole)   Serves 8–10

Basic recipes: Tortillas (pages 11–16); Salsa de Jitomate (page 20)

18 corn or 12 wheat flour
tortillas

8 fl oz (240 ml) corn oil

1½ pints (900 ml) Salsa de
Jitomate

a 3 lb (1.3 kg) chicken,
boiled, skinned and boned

2 green peppers, sliced

½ pint (300 ml) soured
cream

1 onion, chopped finely

8 oz (225 g) mild Cheddar
cheese, grated finely

Oven temperature:
Gas Mark 4/350°F/180°C

This easy dish, also known as Moctezuma Pie, is designed to cope with large numbers. It's ideal for a buffet and easy to prepare ahead of time, but remember to save some sauce to pour over it just before serving. The tortillas should be done ahead of time.

Shallow-fry the tortillas in very hot oil for about 30 seconds on each side. Drain them on absorbent kitchen paper and keep them warm until they are all fried. Heat the oven.

Bring the Salsa de Jitomate to the boil. Pour 4 tablespoons (4 × 15 ml spoon) over the bottom of a 12-inch (30 cm) ovenproof dish. Dip a third of the tortillas, one at a time, in the hot sauce and lay them on the bottom of the casserole. Overlap the tortillas so that all are lying flat. Spoon some more of the sauce over the tortillas to cover them, making sure all the edges are well soaked.

Arrange about a third of the chicken pieces on top, followed by the peppers, soured cream and chopped onion; then sprinkle liberally with the grated cheese. Repeat twice, until all the tortillas are used, finishing with soured cream and cheese. If you are using wheat flour tortillas, it is preferable to use only three tortillas per layer and have more layers.

Bake uncovered for 40 minutes and serve hot, accompanied with Frijoles Refritos (page 19), courgettes, a corn or green salad and slices of avocado.

CHILES RELLENOS

(Stuffed peppers)   Serves 6

Basic recipes: Salsa de Jitomate (page 20); Picadillo (page 23), optional

6 medium-size green peppers

8 oz (225 g) mild Cheddar cheese, sliced, or 1 lb (450 g) Picadillo

3 large eggs (size 1–2), separated

8 fl oz (240 ml) cooking oil

8 oz (225 g) plain flour

1½ pints (900 ml) Salsa de Jitomate

Oven temperature:
Gas Mark 4/350°F/180°C

Famous and very traditional, Chiles Rellenos is a hearty main dish. The peppers are filled with either spicy minced beef or cheese, and some of each type are often served at the same meal to give a choice of fillings. In Mexico Poblano peppers are used; they are a darker green and hotter than the capsicums sold in Britain. In order to make the peppers hotter I add green chillies to the sauce. The egg coating method is called 'capear' and is also popular for parboiled cauliflower, broccoli and large courgettes.

Place the peppers on a hot grill, turning them around as the skins blister. Remove each pepper when it is ready and cover with a damp tea-towel for 10–15 minutes. This helps to steam them and to flavour the flesh.

Peel off any burnt skin you can. Cut off the stalks by cutting around them with a sharp knife, then remove the pips. Stuff each pepper with a slice of cheese or 2 tablespoons (2 × 15 ml spoon) Picadillo. Hold the opening together and secure it with a cocktail stick or two. If the pepper breaks anywhere else, hold it together with more cocktail sticks.

Beat the egg whites until they are stiff and beat the yolks until they change colour to a light yellow. Combine the two by stirring the yolk into the white gently.

Heat the oven. Heat the oil in a frying pan. Toss each pepper in the flour, and then dip it into the egg batter and carefully place it in the hot oil. Keep the heat low, as it will burn easily. Until you get more practice, fry only one at a time. Using a kitchen fork and spoon, turn the pepper around until it is golden brown all over. Remove it from the oil and drain on absorbent kitchen paper. Continue until all the peppers are fried.

Put 4 tablespoons (4 × 15 ml spoon) of the tomato sauce in an ovenproof dish and place the fried peppers in it. Pour the rest of the sauce over the peppers and cover the dish with aluminium foil. Bake for about 1 hour. Serve hot, accompanied perhaps by warm, soft tortillas, Guacamole (page 22) and Frijoles Refritos (page 19).

CARNITAS

(Marinated roast pork)   Serves 6

1 onion, chopped

2 cloves of garlic

1 teaspoon (5 ml spoon) salt

½ teaspoon (2.5 ml spoon) ground black pepper

a pinch of sugar

4 tablespoons (4 × 15 ml spoon) malt vinegar

4 lb (1.8 kg) shoulder of pork, cut into 4-inch (10 cm) pieces with all the extra fat removed

1 pint (600 ml) water

1 lb (450 g) lard, cut into cubes

Oven temperature:
Gas Mark 3/325°F/170°C

Carnitas are a typical outdoor meal; they are also the typical take-away Sunday lunch dish and the restaurants selling them are numerous. They are usually eaten wrapped in a warm soft tortilla with various sauces and accompaniments, such as those suggested at the end of this recipe.

Liquidise together the onion, garlic, salt, black pepper, sugar and vinegar in a blender for 40 seconds at high speed. Smooth this paste all over the meat and leave it to marinate overnight or for at least 2 hours.

Heat the oven. Put the meat and marinade in a large casserole dish with the water and lard. Cover and bake in the oven for about 2 hours, basting and turning occasionally. Uncover and cook for a further half hour, turning once, until the meat is golden brown all over.

Drain off the extra fat. Pour the concentrated gravy over the meat and serve hot on a serving dish. Each person can then help himself to a portion and roll it up in a warm tortilla. Serve with sauces like Salcita de Jitomate or Guacamole (page 22) and accompaniments such as Arroz Blanco (page 63), Rajas Encebolladas (page 76) and Frijoles (page 18).

CHILLI CON CARNE

(Spicy meat casserole) Serves 10

Basic recipe: Frijoles (page 18)

2½ lb (1.25 kg) shoulder of pork, cubed

2 tablespoons (2 × 15 ml spoon) malt vinegar

a pinch of sugar

8 tablespoons (8 × 15 ml spoon) cooking oil

2 bay leaves

2 pints (1.2 litres) Frijoles, and their liquid, if any

2 cloves of garlic

2 onions

4 green chillies (fewer for a milder dish)

6 sprigs of fresh coriander

1 teaspoon (5 ml spoon) powdered cinnamon, or a 2-inch (5 cm) piece of cinnamon stick

10 cloves

½ teaspoon (2.5 ml spoon) oregano

½ teaspoon (2.5 ml spoon) marjoram

1 teaspoon (5 ml spoon) sesame seeds

2–4 tablespoons (2–4 × 15 ml spoon) chilli powder

1–2 teaspoons (1–2 × 5 ml spoon) cayenne pepper

6 tablespoons (6 × 15 ml spoon) tomato purée

14 oz (397 g) can of peeled tomatoes, well mashed

salt and black pepper

Chilli con Carne is not really a Mexican dish. Its origins are in Mexico, though, and in all probability it was when the Americans came over the border for Mexican food and were offered the spicy meat dish Mole de Guajolote, accompanied by fried beans and white rice, that they were inspired to try something similar when they went back home. I have included this well-known recipe as well as Mole de Guajolote, as the latter requires a number of ingredients not easily found in this country. Although American Chilli con Carne is generally made with minced beef, cubed pork is more commonly used in Mexico for dishes of this type, as here.

Use the lowest amounts stated below for chilli powder and cayenne pepper the first time you make it, as the higher amounts make a very hot dish, which will appeal only to those who can tolerate such food.

Season the meat with the vinegar, ½ teaspoon (2.5 ml spoon) salt, ¼ teaspoon (1.25 ml spoon) pepper and sugar and leave it to marinate for 20 minutes.

Heat the oil and when it is very hot lightly fry the meat in it. Remove the meat and simmer it with the bay leaves in 2 pints (1.2 litres) water, until tender.

Meanwhile, roughly chop the garlic, onions and chillies. Then put ¼ pint (150 ml) of liquid from the cooked beans, the garlic, onion, chillies, herbs and spices together in a blender and liquidise. Fry the mixture in the remaining oil for about 2 minutes, stirring constantly. Strain the meat, reserving the liquid, and add it to the mixture together with the tomato purée, mashed tomatoes and cooked beans; simmer gently, stirring occasionally so that it does not stick.

In a separate pan, boil the reserved liquid from

the meat until reduced by half, skimming off any foam. Add this to the mixture and simmer for about 15 minutes, to a thick consistency. Serve with Arroz Blanco (page 63), a tossed green salad and warm tortillas. This dish freezes well and can be refrigerated for up to three days.

CAMARONES AL MOJO DE AJO

(Prawns in garlic) Serves 4

2 tablespoons (2 × 15 ml spoon) cooking oil

2 tablespoons (2 × 15 ml spoon) butter or margarine

2 cloves of garlic, chopped very finely

½ medium-size onion, chopped very finely

2 oz (50 g) fresh parsley, chopped finely

1 green chilli, chopped finely (optional)

1 lb (450 g) raw shelled prawns, fresh or thawed from frozen

½ chicken stock cube

juice of ½ lime or lemon

a pinch of ground black pepper

To garnish:

slices of lime or lemon

sprigs of fresh parsley

This dish is delicious and, despite the fact that in Mexico prawns are much bigger, small frozen prawns done in this manner are just as good. The garlic flavour is much milder than you would expect and may even pass unnoticed.

Heat the oil and butter or margarine in a large, heavy frying pan. Add the garlic, onion, chopped parsley and chilli, and fry until the parsley starts to look very dark green and dry.

Add the prawns, crushed stock cube, lime or lemon juice and black pepper. Increase the heat and stir-fry for 3 minutes. Serve individually, garnishing each portion with fresh parsley and slices of lime or lemon. Serve with Arroz Blanco (page 63), Guacamole (page 22) and a green salad.

PESCADO A LA VERACRUZANA

(Fish in a tomato sauce)   Serves 6

Basic recipe: Salsa de Jitomate (page 20)

2½ lb (1.25 kg) haddock fillets

1 lime or lemon, halved

½ teaspoon (2.5 ml spoon) salt

¼ teaspoon (1.25 ml spoon) ground black pepper

1½ pints (900 ml) Salsa de Jitomate

juice of 1 orange

2 red peppers, sliced finely with the seeds removed

1 large onion, sliced finely

18 stuffed olives

2 bay leaves

1 tablespoon (15 ml spoon) capers, drained

4 sprigs of fresh parsley

2 green chillies, whole or sliced finely (optional)

To garnish:

slices of orange

sprigs of parsley

Oven temperature:
Gas Mark 4/350°F/180°C

Veracruz is a very important port in the Gulf of Mexico and is the home of this traditional dish, a blend of Spanish and Mexican cuisine at its best. It is generally made with red snapper, which is found in the Gulf of Mexico and is considered a delicacy; haddock is similar in texture and is used in the recipe here. The capers and olives make it appetising and colourful, and it is an excellent main course for fish lovers.

Heat the oven. Wipe the fish and rub it all over with the lime or lemon. Season it with the salt and pepper. Spoon half of the Salsa into an ovenproof dish and place the fish on top. Add the orange juice, red pepper, onion, olives, bay leaves, capers, sprigs of parsley and chillies and pour the remaining sauce over it.

Cover with foil and bake for 1 hour. To serve, rearrange the pepper slices and the olives so that they show and garnish with the orange slices and sprigs of parsley. Serve with warm, crusty bread or rice and a green vegetable.

Pescado a la Veracruzana; Camarones al Mojo de Ajo

CHILES RELLENOS DE FRIJOL

(Peppers stuffed with beans)   Serves 6

Basic recipe: Frijoles Refritos (page 19)

4 fl oz (110 ml) olive or corn oil

6 medium-size green peppers, stalks and seeds removed

3 large onions, sliced thinly

1½ pints (900 ml) malt vinegar

1 tablespoon (15 ml spoon) sugar

2 green chillies, sliced thinly

2 teaspoons (2 × 5 ml spoon) oregano

1 teaspoon (5 ml spoon) thyme

1 teaspoon (5 ml spoon) cumin

2 bay leaves

½ teaspoon (2.5 ml spoon) salt

¼ teaspoon (1.25 ml spoon) ground black pepper

1¼ lb (550 g) Frijoles Refritos

This dish is delicious and makes a good meatless main course for summer. It must be prepared two days before it is needed, as the peppers need to marinate.

Heat the oil in a large, heavy frying pan and sauté the peppers and onions until the onions turn translucent. Slowly add the vinegar, sugar, chillies, all the spices and seasoning and then simmer until the peppers are soft. Remove the onions and peppers from the liquid and continue simmering until it is reduced by half.

In the meantime, allow the peppers to cool and remove any blistered skin from them (it is not necessary to remove all the skin). Stuff the peppers with the re-fried beans and secure the tops with cocktail sticks if necessary.

Arrange the peppers in a serving dish, placing the onions over them. Then pour the hot spiced vinegar over them. When cool, leave them uncovered in the fridge or a cool place for two days before serving. Try these peppers with Arroz Blanco (page 63), Guacamole (page 20) and warm, soft tortillas.

Arrange the peppers in a serving dish, placing the onions over them. Then pour the hot spiced vinegar over them. When cool, leave them uncovered in the fridge or a cool place for two days before serving. Try these peppers with Arroz Blanco (facing page), Guacamole (page 22) and warm, soft tortillas.

ARROZ BLANCO

(Mexican-style white rice)   Serves 6–8

4 tablespoons (4 × 15 ml spoon) cooking oil

12 oz (350 g) long grain white rice

1½ pints (900 ml) hot water

½ teaspoon (2.5 ml spoon) salt

1 chicken stock cube

2 sprigs of fresh coriander or parsley

1 medium-size onion, chopped finely

2 whole green chillies

1 clove of garlic, skewered on a cocktail stick

Rice was introduced into Mexico by the Spanish and is now grown and eaten in Mexico regularly. When used as a main course, it is cooked with chicken, fish and vegetables. Otherwise it is treated as a side dish. This particular way of cooking rice is suitable for any recipe calling for plain rice and it's great! It's nice and fluffy, it doesn't stick and it's much tastier than plain boiled rice.

Heat the oil in a thick-bottomed pan which has a tight-fitting lid. Add the rice and sauté, stirring continually, for about 4 minutes or until the rice changes colour.

Drain off all the excess oil and then add the water and all the other ingredients. Cover and bring to the boil quickly. Now reduce the heat and simmer, covered, for 15 minutes or until all the water is absorbed; the rice should double in volume and become light and fluffy. Discard the garlic and the cocktail stick, herbs and chillies. Serve hot or cold.

To freeze: cool the rice and store it in an airtight container. To thaw, leave it at room temperature for about 1 hour. To reheat, place the rice in a pan with 2 tablespoons (2 × 15 ml spoon) of water in the bottom, cover and place over a low heat or in a medium hot oven, Gas Mark 4/350°F/180°C, for about 20 minutes.

To make a rice mould: oil a ring mould and press the newly cooked rice gently but firmly into the mould whilst it is still warm. To serve the rice immediately, turn it upside-down on a hot platter and fill the centre with Guacamole (page 22) or Rajas Encebolladas (page 76). To serve the rice later, cover the mould with kitchen foil and place it in a pan of water in a low oven, Gas Mark 2/300°F/150°C, for 30 minutes, then serve as above.

CHILES EN NOGADA

(Stuffed peppers in walnut sauce)   Serves 8

Basic recipe: Picadillo (page 23)

8 green peppers

12 oz (350 g) Picadillo

shredded lettuce

3 oz (75 g) walnuts,
chopped finely

2 oz (50 g) ground almonds

4 oz (100 g) cream cheese

5 fl oz (150 ml) carton of
single cream

1 teaspoon (5 ml spoon)
lemon juice

¼ teaspoon (1.25 ml
spoon) salt

To garnish:

pomegranate kernels
(optional)

7 oz (200 g) can of red
peppers

It is traditional to eat these peppers in early September when the walnuts are green and easy to peel. September is the patriotic month in Mexico and the green, white and red in this dish are said to have been planned to match the colours of the Mexican flag.

Place the peppers on a hot grill, turning them round as the skins blister. Remove each pepper when it is ready and cover with a damp tea-towel for 10–15 minutes. This helps to steam them and to flavour the flesh. Peel off any burnt skin you can. Cut off the stalks by cutting around them with a sharp knife and then remove the seeds. Stuff each pepper with 2 tablespoons (2 × 15 ml spoon) Picadillo. Close the opening and secure if necessary with a cocktail stick or two. If the pepper breaks anywhere else, hold it together with more cocktail sticks. Arrange the peppers on a bed of shredded lettuce.

Mix together the walnut pieces, ground almonds, cream cheese, cream, lemon juice and salt. Pour this mixture over the peppers and decorate with pomegranate kernels, if desired, and strips of canned red pepper. Serve cold with Arroz Blanco (page 63) and salad.

Chiles en Nogada; Arroz Blanco

TORTA DE PESCADO

(Pilchard and potato casserole)   Serves 6

1 lb (450 g) potatoes

2 oz (50 g) margarine

1 chicken stock cube

15 oz (425 g) can of
pilchards in tomato sauce or
2 × 7 oz (198 g) can of
salmon or tuna with
3 tablespoons (3 × 15 ml
spoon) tomato purée

2 small eggs (size 4)

3 sprigs of fresh parsley,
chopped, and extra sprigs to
garnish

2 teaspoons (2 × 5 ml
spoon) baking powder

¼ teaspoon (1.25 ml
spoon) Worcestershire sauce

salt and black pepper

Oven temperature:
Gas Mark 4/350°F/180°C

*A good, nourishing, tasty and economical dish.
Freshly cooked fish or canned tuna or salmon may be
used instead of canned pilchards, but some tomato
purée must then be added.*

Peel and boil the potatoes. When they are soft,
drain and add the margarine, stock cube,
¼ teaspoon (1.25 ml spoon) salt and a pinch of
black pepper and mash the potatoes whilst they
are still hot. Cover them and keep them warm.

Heat the oven. Cut the pilchards, if used, in
half lengthways and remove all the small bones.
Add the eggs, parsley, baking powder and
Worcestershire sauce to the fish and mix well.
Add this to the potato mixture, mix and transfer
to a well-greased ovenproof dish.

Bake for 30–40 minutes or until it browns on
top. Garnish with fresh parsley and serve hot
with cooked vegetables or with sliced tomatoes
and a green salad.

ARROZ POBLANO

(Rice with cream, cheese and peppers)   Serves 10

Basic recipe: Arroz Blanco (page 63)

1 quantity of Arroz Blanco

1 red and 1 green pepper,
halved, deseeded and cut
into strips

5 fl oz (150 ml) carton of
soured cream, diluted with
4 tablespoons (4 × 15 ml
spoon) milk

4 oz (100 g) mild Cheddar
cheese, grated finely

Oven temperature:
Gas Mark 4/350°F/180°C

*This dish is made in Mexico from local Poblano
peppers, but the peppers you buy in Britain are an
acceptable substitute. Although it is an excellent way
to use up leftover Arroz Blanco, it is delicious enough
to justify cooking some specially.*

Heat the oven. Lightly grease a rectangular
ovenproof dish, and fill with layers of the
cooked rice, pepper strips, soured cream and
grated cheese. Repeat in that order, finishing
with the cheese on top. Bake on the top shelf of
the oven for 35 minutes or until the cheese
browns. Serve hot.

TACO SHELLS

(Fried tortilla shells) Serves 4

Basic recipes: Tortillas (pages 11–16); Guacamole (page 22)

oil for deep frying

8 corn tortillas

1 lettuce, chopped finely

2 cooked chicken breasts, shredded finely

¼ pint (150 ml) Guacamole

Taco Shells are actually the American adaptation of the Mexican fried Tacos, which are tortillas with a filling rolled into a cigar shape and shallow-fried. Taco Shells are tortillas that are deep-fried in the shape of a horseshoe. This is a very practical shape, especially when you are entertaining large numbers: the filling is put on them after frying. Fresh or frozen tortillas may be used and they can be fried ahead of time. If they are going to be stored for more than an hour, however, it is preferable to let them cool and then keep them in an airtight container.

Heat the oil (at least 4 inches/10 cm deep) in a deep fryer to 400°F/200°C as for chips. Immerse and fry the tortillas two at a time, holding them with kitchen tongs against the side of the fryer so as to resemble a horseshoe (see diagram). After 1½–2 minutes they will have shaped and you can then let go, separate them and turn them to ensure even frying. When they are light brown, drain on absorbent paper until required.

Fill with a combination of chopped lettuce, shredded chicken and 1 tablespoon (15 ml spoon) Guacamole. Other possible fillings are Picadillo (page 23) with chopped lettuce and grated cheese, or Frijoles Refritos (page 19) and Rajas Encebolladas (page 76).

Variations: for cocktail parties, tortillas can be cut into 2½-inch (7.5 cm) circles with a biscuit cutter and then fried and filled in the same way. The cuttings needn't be wasted either, as they can be made into Totopos (page 44).

SALPICÓN

(Shredded cold beef salad)   Serves 4

Basic recipe: Salcita de Jitomate (page 22)

1 lb (450 g) cold roast beef, shredded	*A popular name given to this dish is Ropa Vieja ('tatty clothes').*
½ pint (300 ml) Salcita de Jitomate	Mix the shredded cooked beef with the Salcita, garnish and serve cold with Arroz Blanco (page 63), a tossed green salad and warm, soft tortillas.
To garnish:	You place some of the meat in the centre of a tortilla, roll it up and eat it with the other accompaniments.
onion rings	
slices of lime or lemon	

TOTOPO SALAD

(Green salad with crispy fried tortilla chips)   Serves 4

Basic recipe: Tortillas (pages 11–16)

1 lettuce, shredded finely	*This is a good salad for a light lunch and a good way to use up leftovers the day after the party!*
½ onion, chopped finely	
2 tomatoes, chopped finely	Mix together all the ingredients except the Totopos half an hour before required. Just before serving, add the crisp Totopos and toss lightly. Cut the avocado into wedges and use it and the coriander sprigs as a garnish.
6 sprigs of fresh coriander, chopped finely	
2 green chillies, chopped finely (optional)	
8 oz (225 g) cooked chicken, turkey or beef, or shredded canned tuna fish	
juice of 1 lime or lemon	
½ teaspoon (2.5 ml spoon) salt	
a pinch of freshly ground black pepper	
8 tortillas, cut into small squares and deep-fried (see Totopos recipe on page 44)	
To garnish:	
1 ripe avocado	
sprigs of fresh coriander	

Totopo Salad; Salpicón

EMPANADAS

Basic recipe: Picadillo (page 23)

6 oz (175 g) self-raising flour

a pinch of salt

2 oz (50 g) margarine, cubed

2 oz (50 g) lard, cubed

½ teaspoon (2.5 ml spoon) fresh lime or lemon juice

3 fl oz (80 ml) cold water

beaten egg or milk, to glaze

For the filling:

12 oz (350 g) Picadillo

Oven temperature:
Gas Mark 7/425°F/220°C

Empanadas are another good example of the influence of Spain on Mexican cuisine. They are popular throughout Latin America; the name is the same everywhere, but the fillings vary from savoury to sweet.

Sift the flour and salt together and toss the fats in the flour until well coated. Using a spatula, mix the lime or lemon juice and water into the flour without breaking the lumps. Now add just enough extra liquid to bind the ingredients into a soft dough.

With floured fingers, form the dough into a soft ball, place on a well-floured board and shape it into a rectangle about 1 inch (2.5 cm) thick. With a floured rolling pin and short strokes, roll out the dough to a rectangle about ½ inch (1 cm) thick.

With a knife, lightly mark two horizontal lines, dividing the dough into three equal parts. Fold the lower third up over the centre and the top third down over the other two, trapping as much air as possible. Seal the sides together by pressing down firmly with the rolling pin. Repeat the rolling and folding three more times, turning the dough a quarter turn each time. Wrap in a polythene bag and chill for at least 1 hour. While it is chilling, prepare the Picadillo, or your own choice of filling, and allow it to cool.

Heat the oven. Roll the pastry to the thickness of a coin and cut to the desired size. A 6-inch (16 cm) saucer is the right size of cutter for main course Empanadas.

Place 3 tablespoons (3 × 15 ml spoon) filling in the centre of each circle; dampen the edges of the dough with water, fold over and seal together. Place on a baking tray, brush with the egg or milk and prick once with a fork. Bake for about 15 minutes. When they are golden, cool on a wire rack or serve hot. (In Mexico they also shallow-fry them instead of baking but with the extra taste come the extra calories!) Try them accompanied by Arroz con Jitomate and Esquites (see following recipes).

Variation: using a teacup as a cutter and proportionally less filling you can make delightful party-size Empanadas.

ARROZ CON JITOMATE

(Tomato rice)   Serves 8

4 tablespoons (4 × 15 ml spoon) cooking oil

1 clove of garlic

12 oz (350 g) long grain white rice

6 tablespoons (6 × 15 ml spoon) tomato purée

1 teaspoon (5 ml spoon) salt

2 chicken stock cubes

4 sprigs of fresh parsley or coriander

1 medium-size onion, chopped finely

2 green chillies

4 oz (100 g) fresh or frozen peas

4 oz (100 g) fresh or frozen sweetcorn

4 oz (100 g) fresh or frozen diced carrots

1¾ pints (1 litre) hot water

This rice is traditionally made with fresh ripe tomatoes which have been charred, peeled and mashed, but I prefer to use tomato purée for convenience.

Heat the oil in a heavy saucepan with a close-fitting lid and fry the garlic clove until it is dark golden. Add the rice and fry, stirring frequently, until it too is golden or has absorbed all the oil. Discard the garlic clove.

Add the tomato purée and stir for 1 minute; then add all the other ingredients and stir. Bring to the boil quickly and then lower the heat, stir and cover. Simmer for 30 minutes or until all the water has disappeared.

Variation: omit the salt and reduce the amount of tomato purée to 4 tablespoons (4 × 15 ml spoon). For the peas, corn kernels and carrots substitute 8 fl oz (240 ml) cooked beans (see Frijoles recipe, page 18) and ¼ pint (150 ml) of the bean juice. The amount of water should be reduced to 1¼ pints (750 ml).

ESQUITES

(Fried sweetcorn)   Serves 4

| |
2 tablespoons (2 × 15 ml spoon) cooking oil

½ medium-size onion, chopped finely

1 green pepper, de-seeded and cut in thin strips

4 tablespoons (4 × 15 ml spoon) chopped parsley

1 chilli, de-seeded and chopped finely (optional)

12 oz (350 g) fresh or frozen sweetcorn

4 oz (100 g) fresh mushrooms, sliced

1 chicken stock cube

ground black pepper

Fresh corn sliced off the cob is used in many Mexican homes to produce a variety of side dishes. This recipe is traditionally cooked with 'epazote', a herb widely available in Mexico; parsley is an acceptable substitute.

Heat the oil in a frying pan and sauté the onion, pepper, parsley and chilli, if used. Add the sweetcorn, mushroom and crumbled stock cube. Stir, cover and cook over a medium heat for 5 minutes. Uncover and continue frying for 5 minutes more, stirring frequently. Serve hot, sprinkled with a pinch of black pepper.

PASTEL DE ELOTE

(Sweetcorn pudding)   Serves 6

1 lb (450 g) fresh or frozen sweetcorn

4 oz (100 g) butter, softened

4 oz (100 g) granulated sugar

1 teaspoon (5 ml spoon) salt

4 oz (100 g) masa harina (maize flour) or cornflour

1 tablespoon (15 ml spoon) baking powder

3 eggs, separated

Oven temperature:
Gas Mark 3/325°F/170°C

This is a good side-dish, a sort of vegetable Yorkshire pudding. It goes well with chilli sauce or with meat gravy but is more on the sweet side – it reminds me of roasted parsnips. It is a handy way to use corn on the cob which is no longer tender enough to boil.

Heat the oven. Blend the corn kernels to a fine paste in a food processor. Cream the butter and sugar in a bowl until very pale, then add the sweetcorn purée, salt, masa harina or cornflour and baking powder. Beat the egg yolks until they change colour and fold them into the mixture. Beat the egg whites until they form peaks and fold them into the mixture. Turn into a well greased 8-inch (20 cm) square cake tin and bake for about 1 hour. This is a very moist cake which does not rise a lot. Serve hot.

Empanadas; Esquites; Arroz de Jitomate

ENCHILADAS

(Rolled tortillas in tomato sauce)   Serves 6

Basic recipes: Tortillas (pages 11–16); Salsa de Jitomate (page 20)

18 corn or 12 wheat flour tortillas

8 fl oz (240 ml) cooking oil

1½ pints (900 ml) Salsa de Jitomate

8 oz (225 g) crumbly white cheese, such as Wensleydale

2 medium-size onions, chopped finely

Alternative fillings:

4 eggs, scrambled, or 1 whole chicken breast, cooked and shredded

A very popular and traditional dish and very versatile, too. Enchiladas have a filling of chopped raw onions and crumbly white cheese. However, they can be filled with shredded or minced cooked meat or scrambled eggs. The sauces also vary, tomato sauce being the most popular and the easiest to make in Britain. For Enchiladas the tortillas must always be sealed in hot oil first, to prevent them from absorbing too much liquid and becoming mushy. Allow about three small (corn) or two large (wheat flour) tortillas per person. Enchiladas should be eaten hot, immediately after preparation, so this dish is not advisable for large numbers.

Shallow-fry each tortilla in very hot oil for 30 seconds. Drain on absorbent kitchen paper and keep warm until all the tortillas are fried.

Bring the Salsa de Jitomate to boiling point and then keep it on a low heat (if it thickens too much add a little water). To make the first serving, dip one tortilla in the sauce, remove and put it on a warm plate; repeat for two more tortillas. Sprinkle the centre of each of these tortillas with cheese (or one of the alternative fillings) and onion, and roll it up. When all three tortillas have been rolled, spoon more sauce over them and sprinkle with more of the chosen filling and onion. Serve immediately with Frijoles Refritos (page 19) and green salad or Rajas Encebolladas (page 76). Repeat the procedure for the remaining servings.

ROSCA MARGARITA

(Avocado and chicken ring)　　　　　　　　　　　　Serves 10

a little butter, for greasing

6 chicken breasts, cooked, skinned, boned and cubed

8 oz (225 g) Philadelphia soft cheese

½ pint (300 ml) double cream

½ teaspoon (2.5 ml spoon) salt

½ teaspoon (2.5 ml spoon) ground black pepper

4 ripe avocados

2 ripe tomatoes, skinned and seeded

2 green chillies

1 onion, chopped finely

2 tablespoons (2 × 15 ml spoon) olive oil

juice of 1 lime or lemon

1 tablespoon (15 ml spoon) mayonnaise

25 g (1 oz) chopped pecan nuts or flaked almonds

This recipe bears the name of its originator 'Doña Margarita, a very dear friend of mine who was an excellent cook. It is ideal for a buffet because it is so unusual and delicious, and a good talking point.

Butter a 9-inch (23 cm) ring mould. Mix the cubed chicken with the cream cheese, cream and half the salt and pepper. Cut two of the avocados in half and remove the flesh with a tablespoon. Purée the avocado flesh, tomatoes, chillies, onion, olive oil and half the lime or lemon juice in a food processor. Press half the chicken mixture into the ring mould, spoon on the avocado mixture and then the remaining chicken mixture. Press with the back of a wooden spoon to ensure there are no cavities. Cover with cling film and refrigerate for about 2 hours.

Run a spatula round the edge of the dish to loosen the mixture without breaking it, and then invert the mould on to a serving dish. Halve and mash the remaining avocados with the mayonnaise and the remaining juice, salt and pepper and cover the chicken ring with this mixture. Garnish with the chopped pecan nuts or almonds and serve immediately.

RAJAS ENCEBOLLADAS

(Peppers with onion rings)   Serves 6

2 tablespoons (2 × 15 ml spoon) cooking oil

2 large onions, sliced thinly

4 green peppers, cut into strips

4 green chillies, sliced thinly (optional)

3 tablespoons (3 × 15 ml spoon) tomato purée

1 chicken stock cube

¼ teaspoon (1.25 ml spoon) salt

a pinch of ground black pepper

a pinch of sugar

4 sprigs of fresh coriander (optional)

6 fl oz (175 ml) water

½ Camembert cheese, sliced thinly, or 4 oz (100 g) mild Cheddar, grated finely

5 fl oz (150 ml) carton of soured cream

Oven temperature:
Gas Mark 4/350°F/180°C

This is a colourful and tasty side dish, good with Enchiladas (page 74), Carnitas (page 57) and many other dishes. It can be turned into a main dish with the addition of leftover roast pork.

Heat the oven. Heat the oil in a heavy frying pan, add the onions and sauté them until they are soft. Remove the onions and then sauté the peppers until soft. Replace the onions and add the chillies, if used, the tomato purée, crumbled stock cube, salt, pepper, sugar and coriander if available. Add the water, stir and cover. Simmer gently for 5 minutes and then mix in the cheese and cream. Transfer the mixture to an ovenproof dish and bake for 15 minutes or until the cheese melts.

Variation: to make this into a main-course dish in its own right, add 8 oz (225 g) cold roast pork with the cheese and cream before baking. Serve wrapped in soft, warm tortillas.

Rajas Encebolladas

Enchiladas

ole de Guajolote
sca Margarita

MOLE DE GUAJOLOTE

(Turkey in spicy fried chilli sauce)   Serves 12

Basic recipe: Tortillas (pages 11–16)

For the turkey and marinade:

6 lb (2.5 kg) turkey, divided into portions

6 tablespoons (6 × 15 ml spoon) malt vinegar

1½ teaspoons (3 × 2.5 ml spoon) black pepper

1½ teaspoons (3 × 2.5 ml spoon) salt

1 teaspoon (5 ml spoon) sugar

3 cloves of garlic, crushed

For the sauce:

4 oz (100 g) mulato chillies

4 oz (100 g) ancho chillies

4 oz (100 g) pasilla chillies

2 chilpotle chillies

8 tablespoons (8 × 15 ml spoon) oil

2 oz (50 g) sesame seeds, reserving a few to garnish

2 oz (50 g) ground almonds

2 oz (50 g) shelled monkey nuts

2 corn tortillas

3 cloves of garlic, crushed

6 black peppercorns

12 cloves

½ teaspoon (2.5 ml spoon) aniseed

½ teaspoon (2.5 ml spoon) ground cinnamon

Mole *or* molli, *which is the original Indian word, means sauce. This sauce is very rich and is often called chocolate sauce. The misconception comes from the fact that a little chocolate is added to darken the sauce, which is already a very dark red – and does not mean that the turkey is cooked in a chocolate sauce at all.*

Molli is a traditional Mexican dish, and is extremely hot. It is strongly recommended that you use only a quarter of the suggested amount of chillies to begin with, unless you can tolerate such food. Increasing the amount of tomato purée and adding soured cream will also reduce heat.

If you have difficulty in finding the Mexican dry chillies, approx. 4 tablespoons (4 × 15 ml spoon) chilli powder can be substituted, but the taste will obviously not be as authentic.

Because molli is a complicated dish, it is often adulterated and has found many other ways of appearing at our table. One well known derivative is the American chilli con carne. I prefer to call this dish molli because of the surprise in people's faces when they ask 'Do you actually eat moles in Mexico?'

Molli is to Mexico what curry is to India. We always serve it at special occasions as a celebration dish. Turkey, being a native of the Americas, is the meat most appreciated in this dish, but pork and chicken are also quite delicious cooked in this manner. Start preparations a day or two in advance. Molli will keep in the fridge for 10 days and freezes very well. Leftovers can also be used to fill Enchiladas (page 74).

Wash and trim the turkey pieces and sprinkle them with the vinegar, pepper, salt, sugar and the garlic. Marinate overnight in the fridge.

Heat the dried chillies in a heavy-based frying pan for about 3 minutes until they become soft and pliable (the aroma will be quite pungent, so keep a window open!). Discard the stems and

3 onions, quartered

5 tablespoons (5 × 15 ml spoon) tomato purée

2 chicken stock cubes

1 oz (25 g) plain chocolate, grated

seeds and soak overnight in 1½ pints (900 ml) of water.

In the morning, heat the oil and fry the turkey portions (reserving the marinade) until golden. Drain and reserve the oil. Place the turkey with its marinade in a casserole and add 2½ pints (1.5 litres) of water. Boil for about 1½ hours until the meat is very tender. Cool and remove the skin and bones if you wish.

Roast the sesame seeds, almonds and monkey nuts in a dry frying pan by tossing them over a moderate heat for about 4 minutes. Remove, reserve and then place the tortillas in the pan for about 5 minutes, turning them occasionally until they become hard and brittle. Break them into small pieces. Now place with the soaked chillies and their water, the crushed garlic cloves, all the spices and the onion in a processor and blend at top speed until you have a smooth paste.

Place 2 tablespoons (2 × 15 ml spoon) of the reserved oil in a casserole and fry the mixture for about 5 minutes. Add the tomato purée, crumbled chicken stock cubes, chocolate, and cooked turkey meat with its liquid and simmer gently until the sauce is thick and creamy. As the sauce thickens it might stick to the bottom of the pan, so stir occasionally and keep over a low heat.

Garnish with the reserved sesame seed mixture and serve with white rice, cooked beans and warm soft tortillas.

POSTRES
(Desserts)

In Mexico the main courses are so filling that desserts do not feature heavily. Fresh tropical fruits are often all that is offered, frequently without cream. Water ices of different fruit juices, ice creams and light, sweet milk desserts are also greatly enjoyed. Crystallised pumpkin, sweet potato and *chilacayotl* (known in Britain as 'vegetable spaghetti') are some of the many sweets offered after a meal.

PASTELITOS DE BODA

(Sugared shortbread biscuits or 'wedding cakes')   Makes 40–50 1-inch (2.5 cm) biscuits

8 oz (225 g) butter or margarine

2 oz (50 g) caster sugar

8 oz (225 g) plain flour

4 oz (100 g) cornflour

2 oz (50 g) icing sugar, sieved, or 1 teaspoon (5 ml spoon) powdered cinnamon mixed with 4 oz (100 g) caster sugar

Oven temperature:
Gas Mark 3/325°F/170°C

Pastelitos are traditional wedding sweetmeats and are often coated in icing sugar to match the whiteness of the bride's dress. Similar to shortbread biscuits, they really melt in the mouth and are easy to make.

Heat the oven. Cream the butter or margarine with the caster sugar until white and shiny. Sieve the plain flour and cornflour together, then gradually work them into the creamed mixture with a wooden spoon. Knead until smooth.

Take about 1 heaped teaspoon (2 × 5 ml spoon) of the mixture at a time and roll it in the palm of your hand. Arrange the little balls on a greased baking tray and bake for 30–40 minutes until they are pale golden.

Whilst the biscuits are still warm, toss them in the icing sugar or cinnamon and sugar and then leave to cool on a wire rack.

Dulce de Chocolate con Canela; Pastelitos de Boda

DULCE DE CHOCOLATE CON CANELA

(Chocolate and cinnamon blancmange)   Serves 4

1 pint (600 ml) milk

6 oz (175 g) granulated sugar

2 oz (50 g) cornflour

2 oz (50 g) plain cocoa powder

1 teaspoon (5 ml spoon) powdered cinnamon

1 oz (25 g) chopped nuts (optional)

Although chocolate is more popular in Mexico as a drink than as a dessert, this is still a dessert with a distinctly Mexican flavour. It is a simple blancmange-style sweet, served cold in Mexico but just as nice hot on a British winter's day. It takes only a few minutes to prepare, and is also very good with vanilla ice cream.

Put everything except the nuts in a blender and blend at top speed for 45 seconds. Pour the mixture into a saucepan over a low heat, stirring briskly with a wire whisk for about 4 minutes until it starts to thicken.

Before it comes to the boil, sieve into a pudding bowl as quickly as possible to remove any lumps. Garnish with chopped nuts if desired and serve hot or cold with or without ice cream.

ENSALADA DE FRUTA TROPICAL

(Tropical fruit salad)   Serves 6

Pictured on the back cover

*4 oz (100 g) fresh
strawberries*

*½ cantaloupe or honeydew
melon*

8 oz (225 g) water-melon

1 mango

*½ small fresh pineapple or
7 oz (198 g) can of
pineapple chunks in syrup*

*14½ oz (400 g) can of
guavas in syrup*

*juice and slivered rind of
1 lemon*

*6 oz (175 g) granulated
sugar*

*¼ pint (150 ml) water
(omit if canned pineapple is
used)*

*Cantaloupe melons, water-melon, plums, pineapple,
guavas and paw-paw are all very popular fruits in
Mexico and are eaten on their own with a little sugar.
Few desserts, however, are more appetising than a
tropical fruit salad. In Mexico it is always served
refrigerated and is often garnished with chopped pecan
nuts instead of cream. If any fruit in this recipe is not
available, you can either use larger quantities of any of
the others or substitute oranges, bananas, passion fruit
or peeled grapes. Other exotic possibilities are paw-
paw and prickly pear.*

Halve the strawberries and put in a heat-resistant
bowl. Cut the melon into the bowl, putting the
pips and veins in a saucepan. Discard the peel
and seeds of the water-melon, and cube the flesh
into the bowl. Cut the mango as near to the
centre of the stone as possible on both sides and
cube the flesh into the bowl; extract any juice left
in the skins, scraping with a knife if necessary,
and add to the saucepan. Core the pineapple if
fresh and add the core to the saucepan, cubing
the flesh into the bowl; if canned pineapple is
used, drain the syrup into the saucepan and add
the chunks to the bowl. Drain the guava syrup
into the pan likewise; cut the fruit into four and
mix with the other fruit in the bowl.

Add the lemon juice and rind, sugar and water
(if necessary) to the saucepan. Dissolve the sugar
over a gentle heat and then bring to the boil. Boil
for 2 minutes and then pour the liquid over the
fruit through a strainer. Allow the bowl to cool
and then refrigerate.

HELADO DE MANGO

(Mango ice cream)   Makes 4 pints (2.25 litres); serves 12

14 oz (397 g) can of evaporated milk

5 oz (150 g) icing sugar

1 tablespoon (15 ml spoon) lemon juice

1½ pints (900 ml) mango or other fruit purée, chilled

A very different, very colourful and flavoursome ice cream. It can be made with any fruit purée: mangoes are my favourite, but raspberries and strawberries are delicious, too. You have to begin this dish at least two days before it is needed.

Remove the label from the can of evaporated milk and place unopened in a deep saucepan. Cover with water to 3 inches (8 cm) above the can. Bring to the boil and simmer for 15 minutes. Allow the canned milk to cool for at least 2 hours and then refrigerate it, still unopened, for 24 hours. (Do *not* open the can while hot.)

The next day, empty the can of evaporated milk into a very cold bowl and whisk with an electric mixer at top speed for about 5 minutes, until it thickens into a cream and more than doubles in bulk. Add the sugar, lemon juice and chilled fruit purée and mix at the lowest speed just until the fruit is well mixed into the cream. Pour into a chilled container, seal and freeze for at least 12 hours. It is best thawed in the fridge for about half an hour before use.

Helado de Mango

PIÑA VIRREYNAL

(Viceroy pineapple)

14 oz (397 g) can of sweetened condensed milk

1 medium-size fresh pineapple, or 1 lb 13 oz (822 g) can of pineapple chunks, drained

6 fl oz (175 ml) dark rum or tequila

3 oz (75 g) icing sugar

2 packets of sponge fingers (approx. 36 fingers in all)

5 fl oz (150 ml) carton of double cream, whipped

To garnish:

kernels of 1 pomegranate or 2 oz (50 g) sliced almonds

During the 300 years that Spain had Mexico under its domain the Viceroys lived in great opulence and enjoyed the best food the country had to offer. This dessert is the Mexican answer to the British trifle. Sweet, cool and with a nicy rummy flavour, it is good in summer. If you double the amounts, it is easy and colourful for a party. Preparation starts the day before.

Place the unopened can of sweetened condensed milk in a saucepan of cold water, bring to the boil and boil for 2 hours, topping up with boiling water if necessary. Remove from the water, cool and refrigerate, still unopened.

The next day, peel, core and cut the pineapple into bite-size pieces, if a fresh one is used. Put the pieces or chunks in a bowl and pour the rum or tequila and the icing sugar over them; leave to soak for half an hour. Line the sides and base of a dish, 8 × 8 × 2 inches (20 × 20 × 5 cm), with the sponge fingers, dipping them briefly in the pineapple mixture first. (Halve them to line the sides.) Spread the pineapple and juice evenly over the sponge fingers.

Open the chilled can of condensed milk and whip it with an electric mixer for 5 minutes, until it is light and fluffy. Add the whipped double cream and mix. Spread this mixture evenly over the pineapple. Garnish with pomegranate kernels or sliced almonds and refrigerate until needed.

CHONGOS ZAMORANOS

(Curds in syrup)   Serves 6

4 pints (2.5 litres) milk

12 oz (350 g) granulated sugar

5 teaspoons (5 × 5 ml spoon) rennet essence

6-inch (15 cm) piece of cinnamon stick

Despite its unattractive English name (the Spanish means 'little knots from Zamora'), this is one of my favourite desserts. Sweet and chewy with a tang of cinnamon, it is very popular throughout Mexico.

Heat the milk and sugar in a saucepan to body temperature, 98°F/36°C, then stir in the rennet essence. Leave overnight in a warm place until set (it sets like jelly and looks quite firm).

The next day, cut the curd into 1-inch (2.5 cm) squares with a very pointed knife. Break the cinnamon stick into small pieces and insert a piece into each square.

Now simmer for 4 hours on the lowest possible heat. It must only just bubble, because the curds disintegrate easily if boiled hard. After 4 hours remove the curds, then boil the liquid quickly for 15 minutes until it reduces by half. Pour the syrup over the curds and allow to cool. Refrigerate and serve cold.

DULCE DE CALABAZA EN TACHA

(Stewed pumpkin in sugar syrup)   Serves 6

2 pints (1.2 litres) water

juice and coarsely chopped rind of 2 oranges

1½ lb (675 g) raw pumpkin, cut into six and punctured on all sides with a fork

1½ lb (675 g) granulated or muscovado sugar

4-inch (8 cm) piece of cinnamon stick, or 2 teaspoons (2 × 5 ml spoon) powdered cinnamon

In Mexico, pumpkin is mostly eaten as a dessert, not a vegetable. Try both ways of making this dessert – with granulated sugar and with muscovado sugar. The flavours are quite different.

Place the water in a 5-pint (3-litre) saucepan and add the orange juice and rind. Boil until the rind is soft. Add the pumpkin, sugar and cinnamon. Simmer until the pumpkin is soft. Remove it and boil the remaining mixture for another 30–40 minutes or until it is reduced to half the original amount. Return the pumpkin to the syrup and simmer for a further 5 minutes. Remove the cinnamon stick if used. Allow to cool and then refrigerate. Serve well chilled.

BUÑUELOS

(Crispy pancakes with sugar and cinnamon)   Serves 4

Basic recipe: Tortillas (pages 11–16)

oil for deep frying

4 fresh or frozen wheat flour tortillas

4 oz (100 g) caster sugar

1 teaspoon (5 ml spoon) powdered cinnamon

Buñuelos, which originated in southern Mexico, are especially good with a warm muscovado sugar syrup. There are many ways of preparing them, some of which are too complicated and time-consuming. The one I have chosen for this book is a very practical and tasty recipe which is eaten mainly in the north and is very good with coffee or as a sweet biscuit for tea-time.

Heat the oil to about 375°F/190°C. Defrost the tortillas for 20 minutes if they are frozen. Cut each tortilla into 8 pieces. Immerse half of the tortillas (16 pieces) at a time in the hot oil for about 1 minute, stirring occasionally so that they brown evenly. Put the caster sugar and cinnamon in a paper bag. When the tortillas are golden brown, remove with a slotted spoon and shake each batch gently in the paper bag. Arrange on a plate and serve when cool.

Dulce de Calabaza en Tacha; Chocolate Caliente (see page 93)

CAJETA

(Milk caramel)   Serves 8

2 pints (1.2 litres) milk

12 oz (350 g) granulated sugar

¼ teaspoon (1.25 ml spoon) bicarbonate of soda

½ teaspoon (2.5 ml spoon) powdered cinnamon, or 5-inch (10 cm) piece of cinnamon stick

This treacle-like mixture is very popular. Traditionally made from goat's milk, it is sold commercially in large jars. The children fill their spoons and then lick them at leisure! It is also served on vanilla ice cream or can be mixed with a little rum as a filling for French crêpes, garnished with chopped nuts.

Place ½ pint (300 ml) of the milk and all the sugar in a 4-pint (2.25-litre) saucepan and bring to the boil. Simmer for about 20 minutes until the milk goes a rich brown, then remove from the heat.

Pour the rest of the milk into another saucepan with the bicarbonate of soda and cinnamon and bring to the boil. Then add this very, very slowly (it rises very fast) to the sugar and milk mixture, and stir or whip with a wire whisk for a few minutes to dissolve any sugar specks.

Place the mixture back on a low heat, skim any froth that comes to the surface, and simmer, stirring only occasionally, for 1 hour or more, until it reaches 225°F/120°C on a sugar thermometer. Pour into a warmed, clean jar and allow to cool. Eat cold with sweet biscuits or use as suggested above.

BEBIDAS
(Drinks)

Mexicans love hot chocolate – but they are also very fond of fresh, cool fruit drinks, which are always on the Mexican table. Limeade, made with the juice of freshly squeezed limes, orangeade, diluted grapefruit or pineapple juice and sorrel water, a brilliant red tea made with a wild blossom, are all very popular. The colours of such drinks range from white through to a dark brown, which is obtained from the bitter-sweet tamarind fruit.

Mexico has, of course, made its name with the famous aperitif tequila, known as 'fire water', which is always accompanied by lime juice and salt to extinguish the fire! A well-known tequila manufacturer in Mexico recommends the lime first, then salt and finally a one-ounce shot of tequila, but customs vary and so you should experiment to see in which order you like them best.

I should also mention *Cafe de Olla*, or Mexican coffee. Coffee is drunk mostly black in rural Mexico, the beans having been gathered in the wild or grown on home allotments and then home roasted. They are often not of very good quality and the addition of raw cane sugar (muscovado) and cinnamon to the boiling coffee disguises any impurities and turns it into a quite delicious drink.

MARGARITAS

(Tequila cocktails)   Serves 2

1 lime or lemon
salt
4 fl oz (110 ml) white tequila
2 tablespoons (2 × 15 ml spoon) Triple Sec or Cointreau
4 ice cubes

The most popular cocktail with a real Mexican bang. It always surprises the uninitiated as the taste of the salted rim of the glass hits them first. In fact, it is a very practical way of serving tequila, which would otherwise be served with quartered limes and coarse salt.

Halve the lime or lemon and rub the rim of each cocktail glass with one of the halves. Then dip each glass into a saucer full of the salt and chill the glass in the refrigerator.

Squeeze out the juice of the other half of the lime or lemon and blend at high speed for 30 seconds with the tequila, liqueur and ice cubes. Pour into the chilled glasses and serve. (It is not advisable to prepare Margaritas more than half an hour ahead of time, because the lime goes bitter.)

PONCHE DE TEQUILA

(Tequila party punch)   Makes 20 drinks

1 large bottle (750 ml) tequila
8 oz (225 g) granulated sugar
juice of 6 oranges
juice of 6 limes or lemons
2 × 500 ml bottles of American dry ginger
2 × 500 ml bottles of soda water
40 ice cubes

Tequila has the advantage over other drinks of getting parties going very soon after people arrive. It is very strong and breaks the ice, so to speak, almost immediately. In fact the tequila that is exported has to be made separately, as the Mexican proof is too high for other countries! This punch can be prepared before the party starts, while you're still capable!

Mix all the ingredients except the ice together vigorously and chill for 1 hour. Put 2 ice cubes in each glass and pour the punch over them.

CAFE DE OLLA

(Mexican coffee)   Serves 2

4-inch (10 cm) piece of
cinnamon stick, or
½ teaspoon (2.5 ml spoon)
powdered cinnamon

4 teaspoons (4 × 5 ml
spoon) muscovado sugar

3 tablespoons (3 × 15 ml
spoon) water

*Cafe de Olla is popular amongst the Mexican
peasants, who brew it in earthenware pots and serve it
in small earthenware mugs. It is a convenient way of
using any leftover coffee. Although the coffee is
generally boiled with the sugar and the cinnamon, this
method often makes it go bitter, and so I prefer to make
the syrup separately and add it to the coffee as desired.*

Boil all the ingredients together for 3 minutes
and pour into hot coffee or serve hot in a separate
jug.

CHOCOLATE CALIENTE

(Mexican hot chocolate)   Serves 4

4 oz (100 g) plain chocolate
or unsweetened cooking
chocolate, grated

1 pint (600 ml) milk

2 oz (50 g) granulated sugar

2 drops of vanilla essence

1 tablespoon (15 ml spoon)
cornflour

4 tablespoons (4 × 15 ml
spoon) cold water

a sprinkling of powdered
cinnamon

*A drink given daily to children for breakfast and
supper. Traditionally it is drunk hot after being
whisked with a 'molinillo'. This very typical
Mexican kitchen utensil is a type of wooden whisk,
carved all in one piece, with rings carved out of it in
different sizes (one is in the picture on page 9).*

Place the chocolate, milk, sugar and vanilla in a
saucepan and warm gently, stirring constantly.
Do not allow it to boil. Dissolve the cornflour in
the cold water and add slowly to the milk,
stirring constantly. Give it a good whisk to form
bubbles and serve hot, sprinkled with the
ground cinnamon.

ROMPOPE

(Advocaat) Serves 6

14 oz (400 g) can of
sweetened condensed milk

½ pint (300 ml) milk,
chilled

4 egg yolks

¼ teaspoon (1.25 ml
spoon) vanilla essence

¼ pint (150 ml) vodka

¼ teaspoon (1.25 ml
spoon) powdered cinnamon

All Mexicans love Rompope. Traditionally it was made by the nuns of Santa Clara Convent and to this day the most famous Rompope bears that name. Because egg whites were used by the Spaniards to paste gold leaf on to church altars, there appears to be a never-ending number of recipes calling for egg yolks in the Mexican kitchen. The drink is delicious when well chilled and keeps very well in the refrigerator for up to one week.

Place all the ingredients in the liquidiser except the cinnamon. Mix at top speed for 45 seconds. Strain into a jug and cool. Pour into glasses and sprinkle with the powdered cinnamon.

LIMONADA

(Lemonade) Makes about 1¾ pints (1 litre); serves 6

1 large lemon, quartered

approx. 7 oz (200 g) sugar,
to taste

2 pints (1.2 litres) cold
water

ice cubes

To garnish:

fresh mint or parsley

Fresh lemonade is as common to Mexico as orange squash is to England. Since citrus fruits grow abundantly there is always a large jug of 'ade' on the table to quench the thirst in the middle of the hot day. This recipe is a wonderfully fresh drink, delicately scented with the oils of the lemon skin and quite like the real lime juice which we drink in Mexico. Limes must not be used, however, because they become bitter.

Place the lemon quarters, skin and all, in a liquidiser and cover with the sugar and half the water. Liquidise at top speed for 45 seconds and strain into a water jug. Now pour the other half of the water through the strainer to wash off any flavour left. Add a few ice cubes and garnish with a little fresh mint or parsley. Serve chilled.

INDEX TO RECIPES

Recipes are indexed under both Mexican names and English translations.

Design and layout: Ken Vail Graphic Design
Photography: John Lee
Food preparation for photography: Ann Page-Wood
The publishers wish to thank the Mexican Tourist
Council for their help in supplying some of the items
which appear in the photographs.
Illustrations: Mandy Doyle
Typesetting: Westholme Graphics Ltd
Printed and bound by Balding & Mansell Ltd
Wisbech, Cambs